Egyptian Mythology

A Comprehensive Guide to Ancient Egypt

Table of Contents

Introduction 1

Chapter 1: Ancient History of Egypt 3

Chapter 2: The Different Egyptian Gods 21

Chapter 3: The Heroes 38

Chapter 4: The Monsters 56

Chapter 5: Famous Egyptian Mythology Stories 73

Chapter 6: The Book of Thoth and The Book of the Dead 89

Chapter 7: Ancient Sacrifices and Rituals 101

Conclusion 120

Introduction

Congratulations on purchasing *Egyptian Mythology*, and thank you for doing so.

Ancient pyramids. Pharaohs and Gods. Mummies, myths, and magic. There is nothing quite like the wonders and mysteries of the ancient Egyptians. This ancient civilization lasted for over 3,000 years and in that time, became one of history's most powerful and iconic civilizations. Ancient Egypt is easily one of the most influential societies to ever exist in this world, so powerful that we still think about it and talk about it today. You may not recognize any Assyrian Kings or comprehend the Assyrian language, but you would have heard of King Tut and Cleopatra. You may even recognize the Eye of Horus.

When you think of ancient civilizations, none are more talked about, thought about, or referenced than ancient Egypt. The pyramids are part of the seven wonders of the world and serve as a constant reminder of the ancient society that was once mighty. As the civilization began to blossom a long time ago along the banks of the infamous Nile river, so too did rich mythology of fables and beliefs. Out of all the ancient civilizations in history, none were more fascinated by the mysteries of death than the Egyptians. During their time, enthralling stories of Gods and myths became the epicenter of their society.

The rulers of Egypt were considered protectors of the people, and they served as divine liaisons between humanity and the many Gods that they worshipped. Let's dive into this rich and fascinating world that may be long gone but is certainly not forgotten!

Thanks again for choosing this book! Every effort was made to ensure it is full of as much useful information as possible, please enjoy!

Chapter 1: Ancient History of Egypt

Pyramids. The Desert. The long and impressive Nile river. These are the images that most often spring to mind when Ancient Egypt is talked about. Let's start by talking about the vast sea of sand known as the Sahara Desert, a place in the north of Africa. Thousands of years ago, there was an abundance of rain in the heart of Africa, and little by little a flow of water was created, and gradually it started to grow. These waters became one of the largest rivers in the world, called the Nile. Many people have settled near this river, but living by the Nile has its ups and downs. In the wet season, the Nile grows so much that all lands around it are flooded, but when the water retreats, the land is ideal for farming since the riverbed has fertilized the surrounding soil. Thousands of years ago, people that had been nomads started building their homes around the Nile; this is how ancient Egypt was born.

The Egyptians learned how to grow crops on rich and fertile land. The food was plentiful. This meant that instead of traveling in search of food, the Egyptian people could stay in one place farming all the food they needed. Egyptians were very clever in using the flooding of the Nile to their benefit. They invented an irrigation system that let them grow even more crops. The Nile soon became a large highway where goods and people traveled, trading with each other. This made the

Egyptians quite wealthy with an abundance of food, and the mobility to trade with other people.

Around 3500 BC, the development of trade and agriculture helped some villages on the banks of the Nile become very wealthy and powerful. Important cities started to emerge along the river around 3,000 BC, creating a kingdom that consisted of Upper and Lower Egypt. Pharaohs were created, and that was the beginning of a great Empire that would last for thousands and thousands of years. Ancient Egypt was in a great location, where on one side the huge desert protected them from attacks from the south, and on the other side, the River Nile provided food, trade, and contact with other villages.

As centuries passed, the power of Egyptian pharaohs began to decrease due to innumerable internal fights. They were also dominated at times by powerful neighboring empires. First it was the Persians, then the Macedonians, and finally the Romans. Cleopatra was the last Pharaoh of ancient Egypt; it is said that no man could resist her extraordinary beauty, which was legendary. Mark Antony was a powerful Roman general who was captivated by Cleopatra and believed that their love would bring back the splendor of Egypt. Mark Antony and Cleopatra went to war against the emperor of Rome, Octavian, but Mark Antony and Cleopatra lost, leaving what remained of Egypt in the hands of Octavian and the Roman Empire. The battle happened in the year 29 BC. At that point in time, the

Roman Empire was not only dominating and oppressing Egypt. They were also doing the same to many other cultures who lived along the coast of the Mediterranean Sea.

Although thousands of years have passed, the influence of the Egyptian civilization still remains alive among us, and their colossal monuments remind us of their grandeur and majesty.

The Social Classes

Life during the time of the Pharaohs was surprisingly modern. Men and women enjoyed equality in their law that wouldn't be seen in other civilizations for many centuries to come. In Egypt, the people fell into one of three categories. You were either royalty, a free citizen, or a slave. Social classes in Egypt back then were not like what we think of today. Since money did not exist yet back then, there was technically no such thing as an upper, middle, or lower class the way we identify with today. The vast majority of Egyptians were people who worked on farms.

Maintaining unity was difficult for the Egyptian rulers since they had many enemies that wanted to invade them and strip them of their wealth. The Pharaohs ruled Egypt for more than 3,000 years. For the Egyptians, their social life was akin to that of the Great pyramids of Egypt; the different groups had varying degrees of importance. At the top of the social pyramid was the pharaoh. The pharaohs were like kings. They ruled Egypt, and all the wealth and treasures of the empire were theirs. They were worshipped as gods, but the life of the pharaoh was not simple. At the very top of the social standing was none other than the pharaohs and those who were of royal blood. The pharaoh at that time was considered a god living on earth. His family, who lived in the palace with him, were incredibly privileged, thanks to their close connection to him. It was the job of the pharaoh to maintain order, control the economy, the laws of nature, the seasons, the flooding of the Nile, the movement of the planets, and more!

The free citizens of Egypt were next on the social hierarchy. The second position of importance on the pyramid after the pharaohs were the priests. Free citizens included the priests, merchants, soldiers, and scribes, traders, farmers, and school craftsmen. Basically, this tier of society consisted of anyone who wasn't born into royalty but was considered free by the laws of Egypt. The priests' main activities were serving the gods in each of the temples and performing offerings and rituals. Below the priests were the scribes whose ability was revered. In ancient Egypt, the very few people who were taught how to write were considered privileged, and that gave them a lot of power in Egypt. They wrote using sacred signs called hieroglyphics. Hieroglyphics were drawings that represented sounds like the modern-day Alphabet, except it was a lot harder to write. There were more than 700 different symbols. The next place on the pyramid was occupied by the soldiers. Soldiers were tasked with protecting the kingdom because Egypt was so rich that many armies wanted to conquer it and take its wealth. After many encounters and many battles fought, the Egyptian army perfected its techniques and became very powerful. The Egyptian army set out to conquer other territories to the East and to the South. In ancient Egypt, there was always something to be done. When officers had no enemies to confront, they were devoted to tasks like digging irrigation canals and transporting blocks of stone to the building sites of the great pyramids.

Finally, at the bottom of the pyramid were traders and craftsmen. Those included in the hierarchy were serfs and slaves. They had no rights, and many who were in this group were captured war prisoners. Although they were at the bottom, the slaves held up the whole pyramid of Egyptian society in many ways. Because of the slaves, the great pyramids were able to be built. The pyramids hold great mysteries and questions that even today remain unanswered. Even modern engineers have a hard time figuring out how exactly they were constructed.

Egyptian Artwork

Ancient Egyptian artwork has a very distinctive look that is unlike any other culture in the world. The ancient Egyptians left behind many works that are treasured today by Egyptian artists. The old artwork was not just created to capture the beauty in their artwork, but to describe a part of life. Beauty was less important to them than the perfection of detail. Egyptians had very strict guidelines for representing different parts of the body. For instance, since human heads can be easily observed from the side, the Egyptians always painted them facing sideways. The eyes were better represented as if the character was facing us, so they used eyes which faced forward while the head looked to the side. The chest and shoulders are best shown from the front, but arms and legs show a better sense of movement drawn from the side. These many different angles make Egyptian art look flat and contorted to our modern eyes.

As for the Pharaoh, he may not have been 30 feet tall, but he was the most important person in Egyptian society. Therefore, the Pharaohs were always depicted as larger than everyone else. The larger they were depicted in Egyptian art, the more important they were considered to be.

The Majesty of the Pyramids

The Pharaohs believed in creating works that would proclaim their greatness throughout the ages. Each pharaoh would construct fantastic monuments to either the gods, or themselves. Take the Temple of Karnak, for example, which comprises three sanctuaries. It remains to be one of the most ancient and largest religious complexes in the world! Or take the Pyramid of Khufu, which is by far the largest of the pyramids, and is estimated to have taken more than 23 years of constant work to build!

The pyramids were built for the great Pharaohs and were filled with many artifacts Egyptians believed that they would need when they met the Gods in the afterlife. They could bring along anything they had from the living world, so many of the Pharaohs decided to take this journey well-prepared by taking many treasures and goods with them. The more they took, the more they believed they would have in the afterlife.

There have been some chilling stories associated with ancient Egypt over the years. A good example is the curse of Tutankhamun. When Tutankhamun's tomb was discovered in 1922, there was a blackout in Cairo, and over the years, many mysterious deaths befell the people who were there at the opening of his tomb. Since then, it's been known as the curse of Tutankhamun.

Hieroglyphics proved to be the key to unlocking many of the mysteries of ancient Egypt. After many years of studying, scholar Jean-Francois Champollion finally deciphered the hieroglyphs and stated that each sign corresponded to a sound. This allowed Egyptian hieroglyphs to be translated for the first time. Being able to decipher hieroglyphics meant scientists could now determine the location of King Tut's tomb. This famous pharaoh died when he was 18 years old, and in 1922 Howard Carter opened his tomb; A tomb that was over 3,000 years old! The tombs of Pharaohs often had warnings and curses written on the walls, but Howard Carter and his team ignored the warnings for the sake of science. Despite the Cairo blackout and the mysterious deaths of people who were there when the tomb was first opened, a lot of people still visit the tomb, and today no one really worries about the curse.

Scientists and Astronomers

The Egyptians were great astronomers and scientists. In fact, they created the 365-day calendar, with each day divided into 24 hours. This is the same calendar we use nowadays to identify which day of the week it is.

Out of the scientists of the Egyptian Empire, one stood above the others, and is still known today as *Imhotep the Wise*. Imhotep was the founder of Egyptian medicine, as well as a high priest. In ancient Egypt, doctors were very respected. They used an early form of paper called papyrus to write down medical notes and diagrams. These notes were like a medical textbook that was handed down from generation to generation. Some have survived to this day. From these findings, we know that the ancient Egyptians even had specialist doctors that just dealt with the skin, the bones, teeth, or heart diseases just like we have today. The ancient Egyptian knowledge of the human body was very advanced, and they had hundreds of different kinds of medicine to treat a variety of diseases and ailments. If a patient was really sick and needed surgery, the Egyptians had many instruments used for doing just that. However, Egyptian doctors took care of the dead as well as the living. They invented ways to mummify a dead body, and this was a very important part of Egyptian culture. Much of the study of ancient Egypt has involved unwrapping and studying these preserved mummies.

Farming Was a Way of Life

Like almost every civilization that came before ours, Ancient Egypt was primarily an agrarian society. To *not farm* would be the exception to the rule. It may not sound like the most glamourous occupation, but this is, without a doubt, the very best way for us to understand what life was like for most Egyptians. Farmers also did so much more than just farming.

The Nile river was unbelievably important to the people at this time, and all major cities were built along the Nile. Herodotus, a Greek Historian, once wrote: *"Egypt is the gift* of the Nile." Growing crops was difficult throughout most of human history since they had to rely on rainfall. If the clouds didn't shower the earth, the crops didn't grow.

If the crops didn't grow, they didn't eat. The Egyptians lived in an arid desert, which would usually make farming impossible. Since the Nile ran through Egypt, it flooded life into what would otherwise be an uninhabitable landscape. The Nile was so consistent that Egyptians created their entire calendar around it. There were three seasons called Akhet, Peret, and Shemu. Every year, during Akhet the river would flood, covering the land in 4-million tons of silt. Silt is a dark, high-quality soil that's excellent for growing crops in. During Peret, the flooding would subside, and the farmers could plough and seed the soil. Finally, Shemu was when it was time to harvest all of the crops you had grown that year.

A Different Kind of Currency

In ancient Egypt, people weren't paid for work in the same way we are today. Egyptians didn't have any coins or money, not until after Greek and Roman influence anyway. Workers were most commonly compensated in bread, beer, and sometimes onions. Egyptians didn't have weekends. The only days off you got were public holidays. Conveniently, holidays were usually set on days in which you couldn't work anyway because of the season. There was one remarkably unique perk to being an ancient Egyptian farmer. The perk is that as a farmer, every day you got to bring your pet cat to work!

This lack of a monetary system meant that if you wanted something that you couldn't make at home, you'd need to barter to acquire it. The wheat and produce you grew was your currency. All sorts of vegetables and fruits were grown, but the most abundant plants cultivated were two cereal grains: barley and emmer wheat; ingredients used in beer, and bread. These were the essentials, and they became the basis of the economy. Towards the end of the Egyptian timeline, new grains were introduced like rice and other wheat variations, but for the most part, Egyptians would grow standard wheat and barley crops. If they didn't have the means to own land for farming, they could rent fertile spots near the Nile that were owned by the government or temples. It was the same routine every year as the Nile's rising was predictably consistent. Throughout the flood, it wasn't possible to work the land. Since the Egyptians needed to stay productive during this period, they would construct buildings for the pharaoh, such as pyramids or temples.

The farming process was a family affair. Together, the family would break down the soil with hoes and plow the fields. The actual mechanics of farming were relatively simple as no complex mechanical, or industrial equipment was used. If they had oxen, they would drag a plow through the ground whilst another family member guided them in a straight line. The alternative to plowing with oxen was manpower, where the ground would be plowed by hand. Once the field was plowed, the wife or daughters would then scatter the seeds from baskets. When they had finished, a herd of sheep would follow, burying the seeds with their hooves.

Once this had all been done, it was all about making sure the crops thrived. A lot of the time would be spent in the canals. The canals that carried water to the land were in constant need of repairs. It was essential that they were running optimally because the crops were thirsty and needed a consistent supply of water. No rain and a massive demand for water meant that special tools were built for irrigation.

Cats and Other Pets in The Ancient Kingdom

It's no secret that cats were the most sacred animal in Egyptian society. The people believed that cats were the guardians of the underworld, and thousands of mummified cats have been found throughout history, which only further provides proof of the animal's importance in Egyptian society. As a sacred and revered animal, cats served nobly in many roles. The ancient Egyptians painted many cat murals during their day and bestowed these much-loved creatures with lavish gifts. Cats were held in such high regard that many Egyptians prayed to the animals themselves. The ancient Egyptians considered cats' magical creatures. They believed these animals brought with them good fortune and luck, especially to the people they lived with. They were considered to be creatures akin to the gods and goddesses themselves. Some Egyptians even believed them to be demi-gods. Many cats even joined their masters when they were out on hunting expeditions. The Egyptians greatly admired the intelligence and the skills behind the hunting tactics of the cat.

Some of the gods were depicted as half human and half feline, or it was believed that the gods had the ability to morph into cats if they wanted. Bast, the cat goddess, is one of the most recognizable of the Egyptian gods in history. It is believed she embodies every characteristic thought desirable in a cat. Grace, playfulness, and cunning are just some of her many attributes. Temples built for Bast housed many cats during that time. Anyone who was caught harming this creature was thought to insult the goddess herself. That is why the killing of a cat was punishable by death in ancient Egypt. The ancient Egyptians believed that Bast, the goddess, would turn into a cat to defeat Apophis, the serpent god, and the enemy of the people. The people of Egypt loved these animals so much that when they died, cats were given a proper burial the same way humans were. The family would mourn the death of the cat, and some even had their beloved pets mummified to preserve their body forever. Cats belonging to nobility and royalty were wrapped with the finest linen the family could get and buried with mice, milk, and scented oils.

While cats were probably the most popular pet, they weren't the only animals Egyptians brought onto the farm. Outside of domesticated farm animals, a dog would also be a great companion and beneficial pet. Like cats, dogs were practical. They'd protect the herds of cattle and round them up when needed. There'd typically be a special place around the side of the house where the animals all lived.

What an Egyptian Home Was Like

Houses in ancient Egypt ranged from little reed huts to enormous palaces. Many farmers would live modestly in sunbaked mud-brick houses. There were lots of clever architectural tricks employed to protect the inhabitants from the harsh weather conditions. The desert had wild temperature swings near 0 to 50 degrees Celsius. The shelter would need to protect those living in the house from both extreme heat and borderline freezing cold. The front door would usually face north to take advantage of the breeze throughout the day. At the top of the house were small windows that would keep the house cool by allowing the hot air to rise and escape.

Reed canopies were often propped up on the roof to create some shade. Adults sat and worked under the canopy whilst the children played. These types of houses were built with three or four main rooms. The entrance was usually a room for people to be received. This room was also dedicated to honoring the local god. The next rooms would be a kitchen or storeroom. Some houses had an underground cellar that was used to store food. This hidden room was accessed through a hatch on the ground. The final room would be a bedroom. A family would sleep in the same room on the floor. In terms of furniture, an Egyptian likely owned next to none. Wood was rare and prohibitively expensive; there are not too many trees in the desert.

As for the bathroom, well, both the bathroom and the toilet would be the Nile river, or a pot outside of the house that would be emptied into the Nile river. Outside of the house would be an area where the animals would rest, along with ancient silos full of grain. An Egyptian would own several of these silos as wheat was essential for survival. Every meal featured a grain derived product, and meals often included bread.

Food and Drink

Egyptians consumed a considerable number of calories daily because of the hard work that they did. They had a highly active lifestyle and a diet rich in variety, full of high-quality natural foods. Beer was the most common drink of choice. The Egyptians would drink beer through a straw with almost every meal. Even the *children* drank beer since it was actually safer for them to drink beer rather than water that came from the Nile. Beer was considered a nutritional source at that time. Beer was stored in large pots and spoiled quickly because of the intense heat. Like beer, bread was also a staple of all meals. There was a myriad of different shapes of bread, including pyramids, ovals, hexagons, and even exotic shapes like curvy women and birds. Living in the desert can be problematic when you are trying to prepare food. Sand could blow into the bread as it was being made. Rock fragments could also find their way into bread mixes as stone tools chipped off whilst grains were being ground. Across every Egyptian class, people had terrible teeth because of this.

Meat, however, was scarce and a rare commodity. Since there was still a need for high-quality nutrients and proteins, the Egyptians would occasionally catch some freshwater fish or hunt some wild birds like geese or ducks.

The Lifespan of an Ancient Egyptian

In Egypt, you'd likely live a short but fulfilling life. You'd probably become a grandfather or grandmother in your brief lifetime, but you wouldn't live for very long by today's standards. Many Egyptians died before they even reached 40. The infant mortality rates were also terrible. Diseases were very common as rubbish was just thrown outside of the house or into the Nile directly.

This was the exact same river that they got their drinking water out of. Bathing in the Nile itself was always an issue because it was full of deadly hippos. Disease and Hippos weren't the Nile's only deadly hazards. People often went out for a swim and were snatched by crocodiles, never again to be seen again.

Many farmers also died working on the pyramids due to falling stones and typical injuries they'd experience in a dangerous workplace with sub-par safety precautions. It didn't help that quality medical treatment wasn't available at all. Death itself was a process that was steeped in tradition. Even the poorest received some type of proper burial from their loved ones. They may not have had the full-service mummification of a royal, but bodies were buried in line with tradition, with dignity and respect.

Families usually had several generations living under the same roof. The children would have plenty of free time as only a minuscule fraction of Egypt's kids went to school to learn reading and writing. Education was a privilege reserved only through nepotism or for the rich. Sons were expected to adopt a trade. Daughters would stay home and complete domestic duties and help out on the farm. By the time they were teenagers, Egyptians were considered to be adults. Girls were married around this time typically. Marriages were social contracts rather than a religious ceremony. Being married with children and a full-time farm to manage meant that there really wasn't much time for leisure.

Chapter 2: The Different Egyptian Gods

In the beginning, there was nothing. The universe consisted of a great chaotic ocean, and *Benben* emerged amid this primal chaos. *Benben* was a huge pyramidal mound. Legend has it that there was a lotus flower within *Benben,* and when it blossomed, it brought the Egyptian God *Ra* to the world, and light came with him. On his own, *Ra* generated the first generations of gods. *Shu* and *Tefnut* were the god and goddess of air, and rain, respectively, and when they were born, the universe was enrapt by a vast mass of primordial waters. *Shu* and *Tefnut* plunged into the water to explore its immensity. *Ra* felt panicked after realizing that his children were taking a long time to return and feared that he would not see them again. He sent his best messenger to find them. *Shu* and *Tefnut* returned safe and sound, and *Ra*'s joy was so immense that human beings were born from his tears. After returning, his children, in turn, generated *Geb*, the god of the earth, and *Knut*, the goddess of the sky, and thus the sky and the earth were created.

The great god *Ra* sovereignly ruled the universe's power, and he was awarded the title of the first pharaoh. The god gifted Egypt with several sacred animals like the ox and the lion, but his greatest offering was the creation of the Nile River, for it was around the Nile's shores that men would come together to edify a mighty civilization that glorified the gods. *Ra* had a premonition that his grandchildren would give birth to a new generation of gods. In his premonition, *Ra* foresaw that the new generation of gods would put an end to his reign. Therefore, he forbade the sky and the earth from producing any more offspring. The story goes that *Knut* and *Geb* would disobey *Ra's* orders and, in doing so, produced powerful offspring.

In this chapter we will discuss these offspring, and the most infamous Egyptian gods!

Ra (The Sun God and God of Gods)

It is believed that *Ra* created all life forms on earth by speaking their secret name. That is except for humans. Humans were born from Ra's tears and sweat, according to the story. The Egyptians referred to themselves as the *Cattle of Ra*. He was the god of the Sun, with the Sun being a symbol of birth and energy. The Sun God was very important to the ancient Egyptians. They believed the sun had a direct and powerful effect on their survival. The father of *Shu* and *Tefnut,* Ra also created *Bastet* and *Sekhmet.* Sekhmet was also known as the Eye of *Ra,* having been created by the fire in *Ra's* eye. She was depicted as a lioness that was sent to slaughter the humans who had betrayed *Ra.*

In the underworld, *Ra* would travel on the *Atet,* which were two sun boats. One was called the *Mandjet,* which translates to *The Boat of Millions of Years.* While riding this boat, he would be in his ram-headed form. The other was called the *Mesektet,* which means the *Evening Boat,* and he would ride this with many other deities, including *Sia, Hu,* and *Hecka.*

Legend has it that *Apophis* was a giant snake and the god of chaos who would try to stop the sun boat's journey every night. He attempted to do this either by consuming it or stopping it with a hypnotic stare. *Apophis* was eventually defeated by *Set,* who would sometimes ride the sun boat with *Ra. Ra* was eventually fused with *Amun,* the god of fertility, and so pharaoh's love to call themselves *"the beloved of Amun." Amun-Ra* gained popularity in ancient Egypt when *Ahmose the First* came into power after following the rebellion that took place in Thebes. *Amun-Ra* became the poor people's champion, and his importance within the ancient Egyptian society continued to rise steadily until it reached a point where it was almost as if he was the one and only god in Egypt. The people began to believe that any other gods that existed were merely a manifestation of the great *Amun-Ra.* No other god in ancient Egyptian history was written about quite as much as *Amun-Ra.* His popularity was such that even civilizations outside of Egypt, like Greece, worshipped *Amun-Ra* in their own manifestation of him, where he was known as the Greek god Zeus.

Osiris (God of the Dead)

Osiris was the lord and ruler of the afterlife, and god of the Underworld. In ancient Egyptian mythological beliefs, during Egypt's early history, the gods ruled as Kings on earth. *Osiris* was one of those gods who served as King. He was one of four siblings, two boys, and two girls. He was married to his very clever sister *Isis;* however, his reign would come to an abrupt end when his jealous brother *Seth* attacked and murdered him. In many versions of this story, *Seth* takes it a step further. Not only does he kill his brother *Osiris,* but he also dismembers his body, tearing it into many pieces. *Isis* and her sister *Nephthys* had to search all over Egypt for Osiris's body, and then when they found it, they fixed it and put it back together again. This essentially made him Egypt's first mummy. The two sisters greatly mourned *Osiris,* crying and beating their brows. *Isis,* who was a very powerful goddess known for her intelligence and her knowledge of magic, was able to bring Osiris back to life and conceive a child by him; a child named *Horus. Horus* would eventually grow up and fight his uncle *Seth,* becoming the next divine king when he defeated him. By restoring Osiris's body and then reviving him, *Isis* made it possible for *Osiris* to live on forever as King, but now instead of being a King of the living, he would be a King of the dead in the afterlife.

The story of *Osiris* has classic elements that anyone can understand and relate to. The jealousy between brothers, love, and grief over the death of a loved one. *Osiris* was the first to die and then be revived or reborn into the afterlife. Although his body was damaged, it was restored, making him the first mummy. This became a model for all humans who wanted to live on after death. This is why statues and paintings of *Osiris* show him as if he were wrapped up like a mummy. For people who wanted to live on forever after death, emulating *Osiris* and imitating the process that he went through, was crucial for success. This is why if you could afford it, it was really important to preserve your body through mummification and then to have an elaborate funeral. These funerals included many rituals, as well as women who would mourn you by crying and beating their brows just like *Isis* and *Nephthys* had done for *Osiris*. It was believed that doing these things helped a person make their way to the afterlife and be able to live there forever.

Isis (The Mother Goddess)

The Goddess Isis was worshiped as a primordial goddess in Egypt, ancient Greece, and the wider Mediterranean lands for over 7,000 years. In Egypt, *Isis* was depicted as a very beautiful woman. The symbols associated with *Isis* were the vulture, sparrow, cobra, sycamore tree, and small hawk. Isis represents everything that is to do with aligning with your true purpose, bringing the power of the universe into your life, authenticity, and your divine contribution to humanity and the earth. She is depicted with a throne on her head.

She was likened to many other goddesses, especially by the Greeks, who identified her with *Demeter,* the goddess of agriculture, *Hera,* the wife of Zeus, *Selene,* the goddess of the moon, and even *Aphrodite* the goddess of love and beauty. The parallel with Aphrodite is a little strange considering *Hathor,* the Egyptian goddess of joy, feminine, love, and motherhood appears to be more similar to Aphrodite than Isis is. This is said to be due to some confusion of the role *Isis* played in Egyptian mythos, so the Greeks began to associate Isis with many of the other Egyptian goddesses. When it came to magical powers, no one could match *Isis*. Not even her brother *Osiris,* nor the god *Ra*. She was the goddess of protection, children, nature, the dead, the commoners, and the noble. She was loved by all who worshipped her.

According to legend, *Isis* was the first daughter of *Geb* and *Knut* and was born in the swamps of the Delton. *Isis* had three other siblings named *Osiris, Seth,* and *Nephthys.* Her brother *Osiris* chose her to be his consort, and she reigned alongside him. Together, they would give birth to a son named *Horus.* Her other children were *Bastet* and *Ammit.* Osiris worked to abolish cannibalism and taught the people of Egypt about producing food and crops. *Isis,* alongside *Osiris,* worked hard to establish order among the people. She taught the women of Egypt to grind wheat, weave cloth, and spin flax. She also taught men the art of curing and treating disease. By getting men used to domestic life, *Isis,* in a way, was responsible for the first institutions of marriage during that time. When she found out about the assassination of *Osiris* she was overcome with grief. We are told that she cut off her hair, tore her robes, and set out on a search for the coffer that *Osiris* had been placed into by *Seth* and his conspirators. Legend says that the coffer travelled into the sea from the Nile and washed up under a tamarisk tree on the Phoenician coast. The tree grew so rapidly that the coffer became an embedded part of its trunk.

The King of Byblos ordered the tree to be cut down and used as a pillar in his palace. When this was done, the tree produced such a magnificent scent that it was talked about by all in the kingdom. *Isis heard* the news of this exquisite scent and immediately understood its significance. *Isis* immediately left for Venetia, where she confronted the queen. The queen did not know that this was *Isis,* and she commissioned Isis to care for her newborn son. While in the palace, *Isis* bathed the coffer in tears and hid it in the swamps of Egypt, away from the evil *Seth*. Unfortunately, *Seth* discovered the body of Osiris, and tore it into fourteen pieces, scattering it across the kingdom.

Seth (God of Disorder)

Seth was often depicted as the *"Seth beast,"* an animal that vaguely resembled an anteater. It was common for the gods back then to be depicted as half man and half animal. Sometimes, *Seth* was even depicted as an animal that many of the Egyptians considered "unclean." For example, the pig or the hippopotamus. His nephew *Horus* was *Seth's* greatest enemy in life.

Seth was the son of *Knut*, the sky goddess, and his status was equal to that of his sisters' *Isis* and *Nephthys* and his only brother whom he despised, *Osiris*. It is said that *Nephthys* was actually one of his wives. His rank and strength among the mighty gods would be part of the reason he managed to gather support during his bitter battle and struggles against *Horus*. After being defeated on earth, *Seth* would go on to travel with *Ra*, the Sun God, helping *Ra* fend off the attacks of the serpent god *Apophis*. Because of his immense strength, *Seth* still managed to gather support and devotion among some of the people. The 19th and 20th dynasties 1292 - 1075 BCE was when *Seth* enjoyed the most respect and worship. Still, the people knew that if there was one god that was dangerous to venerate, it was *Seth*. Dynasties that came later would even depict him as a personification of evil.

Nephthys (Goddess of Death)

Nephthys was the goddess of death, the night, and the rivers. One of the daughters of *Knut* and *Geb,* she was *Horus's* nursing mother. She possessed healing capabilities and was considered to be the nurse of the reigning pharaoh himself. Although other goddesses could assume this role too, it was *Nephthys* who was usually portrayed in this function. She was identified with the role of the priestess and was known as *The Lady of the House.*

Nephthys was associated with divine assistance and protective guardianship by the ancient Egyptians. She was the war companion of her husband, *Seth*. In some versions of the story, *Nephthys* was believed to be the mother of *Anubis,* the god of the dead. Depictions of *Nephthys* were typically paired with her sister *Isis,* and both sisters represented the Temple of Pylon. In her funerary role, *Nephthys* was usually depicted as a kite or a woman who had the wings of a falcon. The wings would usually be outstretched as a symbol of protection. *Nephthys* was also considered the unique protector of the Bennu Bird, or the Sacred Phoenix.

Bastet (The Cat Goddess)

Bastet was the cat goddess of fertility, motherhood, and protection of the home. You might know *Bastet* in her more recognizable cat-headed female form. Bastet went through a dramatic transformation three thousand years ago, and this had to happen almost entirely out of necessity. Originally, *Bastet* was depicted as a lion goddess. She had the head of a lioness and the body of a woman. Lions were recognized by the Egyptians for their ferocity and authority, respected and feared. So why did *Bastet* morph from a fierce lion into a cute and cuddly cat?

Ra was arguably one of the most significant of all the Egyptian gods, holding dominion over the sun. *Ra* had dominion of the *Eye of Ra* symbol, and this was a symbol that *Bastet* used to be associated with prior to her transformation. Legend says that *Bastet* had a sister who also looked like a lion. She was named *Sekhmet*. Now, *Sekhmet* was said to be a warrior goddess who was vicious, coming to earth to rid the planet of her enemies and those who would stand against her. While originally the sisters looked identical, there were some significant differences between them. For one, *Bastet* was viewed as being more benevolent and passive compared to her fearsome warrior sister. *Sekhmet* inspired fear, and the differences between the sisters only increased over time. *Bastet* became calmer as the years went by while *Sekhmet* became fiercer. Hieroglyphics throughout history began to depict *Bastet* as having a softer and more nurturing side to her personality. This is what caused her to change from a lion to a cat in their depictions.

Bastet was viewed as a protector and the goddess of fertility too. That's because the Egyptians had an appreciation for the large litter of kittens that each cat could produce. Since the Egyptians too aspired to have as many children as they could, they had great respect for the incredible fertility abilities of the female cat. *Bastet* is sometimes depicted with a litter of kittens around her, presenting fertility and motherhood.

Sekhmet

The sister of *Bastet, Sekhmet,* translates to mean "the powerful one." *Sekhmet* was both a warrior goddess and the goddess of healing. Depicted as a lioness and a fierce hunter, the ancient Egyptians believed that *Sekhmet's* breath was what formed the dessert. She was the protector of the pharaohs, according to the stories, and she led them into warfare. *Sekhmet* was married to *Ptah,* the god of architects and craftsmen. She was considered a solar deity, and sometimes she would be called the daughter of *Ra.* She was often linked with the goddess *Hathor,* who was the goddess of love and motherhood. Her cult was very prominent and dominant, and it is believed that when *Amenemhat I,* the first pharaoh of the 12th dynasty, moved the capital of Egypt to Itj-tawy, the central focus of her cult moved too. She was portrayed as a ferocious lioness. Sometimes she was depicted as half woman and half lioness (body of a woman and head of a lioness). She would be dressed in red, which symbolized the color of blood.

Anubis (The God of the Dead)

Anubis is the god of the dead, and he's also the god of mummification and funeral rites. He is commonly depicted with a jackal's head and a man's body. Why a jackal's head? It's because Egyptians saw jackals scavenging cemeteries and thus associate them with the dead. *Nephthys,* who was the wife of *Seth,* wanted a child so badly, but *Seth* was impotent. So, *Nephthys* disguised herself as *Isis* since it was the only way she could think of to trick *Osiris* into sleeping with her. From their forbidden relations came the god *Anubis. Osiris* loved *Anubis,* and when *Osiris* was killed by *Seth, Anubis* was the one who embalmed his father and worked on turning his corpse into a mummy.

This mummification process inspired the people of Egypt who thought that if it was good enough for the gods, it would be good enough for a man. The story goes that if the corpse is not mummified in the right manner, it would be dug up and devoured by *Anubis*. No one entered the underworld without first being judged by Anubis. He is the embalmer of preserved corpses. He is the final arbiter during the time of the final judgment. He is the keeper of the legendary scales that weigh the weight of a person's *heart*. If a person's heart didn't weigh enough, it was *Anubis* who would cast the person's soul into the deep, dark underworld. The soul would be lost forever, and the person would have no chance of being reborn. There are conflicting stories claiming that either *Ra, Bast,* or *Hesat,* are the rightful parents of *Anubis,* but it is unclear which version of events may have been most widely believed during ancient times.

Amun (The God of Air)

Amun was the god of the air and the king of the Deities. He rose to prominence in the 11th and 16th century BC after he merged with *Ra,* and from that moment on, he became known as *Amun-Ra* or *Amen-Ra*. *Amun* was a patron of the troubled and the poor, and he was the focal point when it came to personal piety. To seek *Amun's* help, one had to first confess their sins.

Ma'at (Goddess of Justice and Truth)

The concept of Ma'at is symbolized by a feather weighed against the heart during judgment, but what was Ma'at really? A feather? A goddess? Truth? Ma'at was a guideline for how to live life and was essential for getting into the afterlife. This is probably the most well-known aspect of Ma'at as a kind of framework for how one should behave and speak, which if followed throughout life, could gain you acceptance into the afterlife.

Ma'at is often translated as truth or justice, but one could argue that divine order is a more accurate translation. Ma'at is often shown as a goddess with a feather on her head. While Ma'at is a concept relating to divine order and truth, the ancient Egyptians also personified Ma'at as a goddess. This is something they often did with concepts, and she's often said to be the daughter of the Sun God Ra. In art, you might see the feather alone to symbolize Ma'at, such as when it is depicted in the weighing of the heart. But often, you'll see her as a full goddess in human form with a feather on her head. In later times, she was often shown with outstretched wings.

Ma'at was considered essential for keeping the world running. It made individuals behave as they should, with a sense of morality. The gods relied on Ma'at, and without it, the world would collapse and return to the dark, chaotic state from before creation.

Hathor (Goddess of Love and Beauty)

Hathor was known by many names. She was important in many aspects of Egyptian life and death. Originally, *Hathor* was depicted as a manifestation of the Milky Way, but this version of the Milky Way was the milk produced from the udders of a heavenly cow. Cows were held in high esteem at the time, and Hathor was often depicted as a cow herself. Hathor would take on many attributes of other goddesses as time went by. The people of Egypt associated beauty, love, motherhood, and sexuality with her. But there was something else she was known for too, and that was *vengeance*. In certain periods in Egyptian history, pharaohs were referred to as *"sons of Hathor."*

Thoth (God of Knowledge and Wisdom)

His name translates to *"He who is like an Ibis."* The Ibis itself was a sacred animal to the ancient Egyptians, and they were popular pets. They represented wisdom, which is one of Thoth's main attributes. The most popular description of his origin is that he was born at the beginning of time itself. He then laid a cosmic egg containing all of creation. Thoth held a prime spot in many of the most popular Egyptian myths and for good reason. He is the god of the moon, the patron of science, literature, inventions, writing, the spokesman and mediator of the gods, as well as the keeper of records.

Thoth was said to have broken the curse Ra placed on Geb and Nut by outsmarting the Sun god, thus allowing Geb and Nut to conceive Isis, Osiris, Nephthys, and Seth. Upon the murder of

Osiris, Thoth remained loyal to him and contributed to his resurrection. Through the trueness of his voice, magic incantations were strengthened and made more effective. He also helped protect the son of Osiris, Horus, by healing his wounds as he grew up. He continued this trend as Horus and Seth were engaged in their eternal battle. He would heal their wounds and advise them both, so that neither had an unfair advantage in their battles.

Thoth's disciples would boast that they had access to his crypt, where he kept all of his books containing the magic needed to control the elements and subdue the gods themselves. Once Thoth had completed his reign on earth, he ascended to the skies where he served other roles, mainly as the protector of the moon. The moon would make its course throughout the month where it was exposed to monsters, and Thoth would protect it from them. Being a lunar deity, he measured time and created the months of the year. He was a regulative force and was in charge of calculations and measurements. He was the keeper of the divine archives and the patron of history.

Sobek (Lord of the Water)

Easily identifiable by his crocodile head, this ancient Egyptian deity offered protection from the dangers of the Nile. While *Sobek* was originally acknowledged as the actual creator of the river and perhaps even of the world, he's primarily associated with fertility. Pharaonic and military power was also in his purview. The ancient Egyptians, according to history, were said to mummify crocs, since they hoped to receive special protection and care from *Sobek* when they moved on into the afterlife.

Chapter 3: The Heroes

Ancient Egypt was the land of the pharaohs, and heroes existed among both gods and men. Egypt has a very long, very old history. Many have become the pharaohs of Egypt throughout the centuries, but none took on the role quite like Ramses II did when he ruled sometime in 1200 BC. He fought many battles, built many temples, produced many children, and quite possibly, his greatest accomplishment was how long he reigned over Egypt. But was Ramses II the only hero in ancient Egypt's rich history? Not at all, but he is one of many that left a legacy so strong it is still talked about to this very day. In this chapter you will discover the story of Ramses II, as well as the stories of the other prominent heroes in ancient Egypt and Egyptian mythology!

Ramesses II

Ramesses was born 30 years after Akhenaten, who was known for being an appalling leader of the people. Ramesses' father was Seti the First. It was his father who would campaign in Levant against the Anatolian Empire of the Hittites. As a young man, Ramesses would serve in his father Seti's army. It is there that he would learn how important it was to pay attention to the northern territories of Egypt. During his reign as pharaoh, Ramesses II would have more than 150 children, many of which he outlived since he went on to live until he was 90 years old. He became the pharaoh in the year 1279, and one of his very first duties was to protect Egypt from the *Sherdons,* which were the pirates of the sea. After ensuring the security of Egypt, Ramesses included the pirates as part of his Army's Royal Guard. The next decade would see Ramesses trying to corral Levant and Canaan, fighting the Hittites. This battle would mark the end of Ramesses' military operations and the beginning of the Hittite Alliance.

Ramesses' final 45 years of being pharaoh were relatively prosperous and peaceful. To the people of Egypt, Ramesses II was a strong leader who got things done. He was a commander to be admired and quite a skilled diplomate. He was one of the more stable Kings of Egypt, and the end of his reign was also the end of the last golden age of the Egyptian dynasty. At least, as far as building projects go.

All the way up and down the Nile, temples that Ramesses didn't even build were emerging, displaying his statues and name. Instead of subsequent pharaohs writing their own name over his (which happened a lot back then) the next nine pharaohs simply cut out the middleman entirely and named themselves Ramesses. More than probably anyone else in Egyptian history, Ramesses II left his mark in stone everywhere. After one fateful and final duel against presumably Anubis himself, Ramesses died at the age of 90. This was after almost 70 years of ruling.

Cleopatra

Besides Ramesses, there's probably no name more famous in ancient Egypt's captivating history than the name Cleopatra. Shakespeare's version of the infamous Cleopatra is that she was the beautiful, desirable queen of Egypt and a true, accomplished master of the art of seduction. In this version it was her rise to power that would eventually crumble her own Empire, before she committed suicide. But that's not quite how the story actually went. Cleopatra's real story is rather less uniformly disparaging and is far more interesting. History's pervasive problem with Egypt's final pharaoh is that she usually plays a side character in Roman history rather than ever being the protagonist in her own right. It also doesn't help that the only historical sources that we have on the matter are from Romans, hence the Rome centrism and the casting of her character as a seductress with a habit of ruining otherwise perfectly blameless great men. So, who is the woman behind the myth? What was her real story?

Cleopatra's story actually starts 300 years earlier. It all began when a Greek man, named Alexander the Great, decided that he would head eastward, beat the Persians, and conquer everything in sight. When he died without a clear line of succession, his generals scrambled to claim their corner of the fragmenting Macedonian Empire. A general named Ptolemy claimed Egypt as his and became King Ptolemy. The Ptolemaic dynasty ruled during the so-called Hellenistic era, where Alexander's successors spread Greek culture out to Syria, Mesopotamia, and Egypt. Although Cleopatra's story takes place along the Nile, the ancestry of the Ptolemaic rulers and the culture they promoted were unmistakably Greek.

Fast forward three centuries, and we have Cleopatra VII and her younger brother Ptolemy XIII. Both lived in the beautiful city of Alexandria, the first-century BCs knowledge capital of the entire Mediterranean world. Between the superbly stocked library and the abundance of mathematicians, poets, scientists, philosophers, and rhetoric, not to mention the fact that she was a princess, the young Cleopatra had the best education possible in the entire Greek world. Unlike a lot of her ancestors, she actually put in the effort. She would have been raised on Homer, Herodotus, Plato, Aristotle, and all the classical philosophical works we now know. Cleopatra wasn't described as spellbindingly gorgeous. But rather, she was captivating. She was known to be the ultimate conversationalist, and that's how she won people over. None of her ancestors before her were exceptionally intelligent, and none of them bothered to even learn how to speak Egyptian, but Cleopatra could charmingly convince anyone of anything in all of the nine different languages she spoke. She was the epitome of beauty and brains at the time.

When Cleopatra's father Ptolemy the 12th died, the throne passed to her prepubescent brother Ptolemy the 13th, and she served as his co-monarch. Interfamilial scheming was no stranger to the Ptolemies, and after a couple of years of power-jockeying between them, Ptolemy made the political and military friends he needed to force Cleopatra into exile. However, at the same time, another much bigger civil war was afoot. Caesar was busy staging a gigantic coup and chasing Pompey across the entire Mediterranean. Pompey had close ties with the Ptolemy siblings on account of business with their father, and Cleopatra's hope was that she could promise Egypt's armies in his fight against Caesar if he kicked out her brother and made her queen. However, King Ptolemy decided that Caesar was a better bet, so he had Pompey killed the second he arrived in Alexandria. Caesar was so angered at being robbed of a victory that he stormed the royal palace. Cleopatra saw an opening and seized it. Strolling into the palace wasn't an option on the count of her still being in exile, so she snuck her way in. This is where stories of her powers of seduction began to blossom. Cleopatra needed an ally, and Caesar realized that she was far more useful to have as an ally than Ptolemy.

Ptolemy and his army blockaded Alexandria, and the new power couple was stuck in a besieged royal palace for six months. Caesar put his neck out by betting on Cleopatra, and Cleopatra was clearly a valuable ally in Caesar's eyes and not just a pretty face and figure. By the time that Caesar's reinforcements arrived to break the siege of Alexandria and defeat Ptolemy's armies, Cleopatra was pregnant. It was true love, and by this point, Caesar had conquered the entire Mediterranean. Instead of immediately going back to Rome to be a dictator, he spent an extra year in Egypt with Cleopatra. When he returned to Rome, he publicly acknowledged Cleopatra's son Caesarion as his child. While Caesarion wasn't in line to gain much in Rome, he would spend the next two decades preparing to become a pharaoh of Egypt. Now the queen of Egypt, Cleopatra wasted no time in carefully tending to a kingdom that its rulers had largely ignored for centuries. As the queen, Cleopatra took on the role of Isis incarnate. Cleopatra had two main roles to fill as the protector of justice and the mother of the people. She made effective use of a strong bureaucracy to make sure the economy ran smoothly. She had to deal with a string of droughts in the early years of her reign that she handled remarkably well. She was also very attentive to the disputes between Greeks and Egyptians. Most civil disturbances stemmed from that simple divide, so Cleopatra presented herself as a queen for both her fellow Greeks and for the population of Egypt.

Meanwhile, Caesar was murdered, and his adopted son and second-in-command hunted down the assassins in Greece. After that, the young Augustus Octavian (Caesar's great-nephew) took command of the west while Marcus Antonius held on to the east, and with it, most of the land and sea that bordered Egypt. As the conventional story goes, Antonius summoned Cleopatra to the Anatolian city of Tarsus, where they fell in love with each other the instant they met, starting a dynasty together. The story of the following decade is a quiet one for Cleopatra and almost solely revolves around her affair with Antonius. She had pretty much everything she wanted, and when Antonius set off to conquer Parthia the next year, she would become Empress of the entire East. Cities were already minting coins with both of their faces on them. Unfortunately, the Parthian campaign was a disaster, and Antonius lost 1/3 of his army just on the retreats. Antonius was starting to become more of a liability. Octavian saw an opportunity here, and he cleverly gave Antonius and option. He sent his long-suffering sister and Antonius' actual Roman wife Octavia to the east, along with 2,000 soldiers. The message he was sending was loud and clear. Reject Cleopatra and accept Roman help or forfeit the army and your wife and keep your Egyptian harlot queen.

Since Cleopatra couldn't afford to lose her allies, she did everything she could to win Antonius over. Cleopatra grew stronger and more interdependent than ever. She was declared queen of Kings, with her son Caesarion proclaimed to be Caesar's rightful heir, declared King of Kings and successor to the throne of Egypt. As for her children with Antonius, Alexander Helios was crowned the King of Armenia, Media, and Parthia. Her other children, Cleopatra and Selini, were given

Crete in Cyrene, while Ptolemy Philadelphus got Vinicius, Syria, and Silesia. Egypt and the Roman East were gone, and in its place was the new Empire of Antonius and Cleopatra together.

Beyond the stories of the many beauty treatments and romanticized versions of her tale told throughout the years, the real Cleopatra is still a hero in ancient Egypt's history. She was a woman who used her genius, her wealth, her power, and to a certain extent, her sexuality to accomplish her many goals throughout her life. She planned carefully and worked hard because she cared, and she achieved some remarkable accomplishments. To this day, she's arguably the most powerful woman in history.

Hatshepsut

Her name may not be as famous as that of Cleopatra, but Hatshepsut was still considered one of Egypt's heroes. Not only was she one of Egypt's most successful rulers in the New Kingdom, with a considerable long-term impact on Egypt's well-being, but she was also arguably Egypt's first female pharaoh. Most intriguingly, a couple of decades after her death, her name was erased from her monuments, and her statues were quite literally defaced. Yet, her rule was a truly exceptional one. She became pharaoh through unconventional means, completed extraordinary feats for the cultural and economic benefit of Egypt, and after her death, her name and entire existence was almost erased from memory. Every part of her life was either an oddity, an exception, or a complete mystery, yet her name and fantastic story were almost lost to time. While some have ascribed this grand erasure to familial rage, Hatshepsut's post-mortem demise was almost entirely due to attempts to clean up the historical narrative to suit the wishes of her successors.

Hatshepsut was born in the late 1500s BC to the pharaoh Thutmose the First, whose accomplishments included military campaigns into Syria and Nubia. Hatshepsut, who was a full royal, married her half-brother Thutmose the 2nd, who was from a different wife who not as royal. Egyptian royalty typically intermarried so as to keep the family line pure, but also, the king practiced mild polygamy and bore children from multiple royal wives. Hatshepsut served as Thutmose the 2nd's queen for the decade and change that he ruled for. Even as queen, she wielded quite a bit of power over Egypt. When Thutmose the 2nd died, the throne passed on to his son and Hatshepsut's stepson, Thutmose the 3rd. The problem was that Thutmose the 3rd was a small child. As such, most of the actual power went back to Hatshepsut, who served officially as his regent. Now, this had happened at several points in the past -- and Egyptian Queens serving as Regents was perfectly fine -- but at some point, the balance of power shifted. Hatshepsut officially declared herself to be the co-pharaoh of Egypt along with her young stepson. In Egyptian culture, the pharaoh is the incarnation of the male god Horus. So, while being the regent for her stepson was completely innocuous, declaring herself a pharaoh was concerning for some people. She dressed in the typical male attire of a pharaoh and even wore a fake beard, but in all surviving writings, she's referred to with grammatically female language. Jeff Francois Champollion, the man who translated hieroglyphics, was confused by this one specific monarch that repeatedly showed up in art and records with female attributes despite the masculine clothing and beard. People argued over this for over a century!

Hatshepsut's most notable accomplishments were achieved through her extensive building program. She built and restored temples all across Egypt, from the furthest reaches of the Nile all the way up into the Levant. In the city of Thebes, the temple complex of Karnak had somewhat fallen into disrepair, and Hatshepsut fixed it. She had a particular fondness for erecting obelisks, and as it happens, the tallest surviving ancient obelisk that we know of is from Hatshepsut's reign. Her most notable accomplishment is her mortuary temple of Djeser-Djeseru, which means "The holiest of holies." She also established trade ties with the lands in and around the Levant, which proved to be quite lucrative for Egypt. Her reign was largely internally and externally peaceful. Like many people who existed before modern-day medicine, Hatshepsut is believed to have died of an infection. After her death, her name, and statues were widely wiped out in an attempt to erase the fact that she ever existed.

King Menes

He was the first ruler that united Egypt, joining the upper and lower kingdoms under one government. He was also known by the name *Narmer*. In a bid to unify the people, he had a very exclusive crown made. The crown was made of both red and white colors and molded together to form a double crown. It was meant to symbolize the union between the nations. King Menes's plan worked, and it wasn't long before the people began referring to both lands as the *"The Two Lands."* Egypt wouldn't have been the Egypt that we all know today if it wasn't for the efforts of King Menes.

Tutankhamun

In ancient Egypt's 18th dynasty, a young 9-year old boy ascended to the throne. His name was Tutankhamun, and he would grow up to become one of Egypt's most famous pharaohs. Commonly referred to as King Tut these days, it was Howard Carter, a British archeologist who made the remarkable discovery of King Tut's remains in the 1920s. He uncovered a tomb that was stunning, to say the least. The tomb was the tomb of a king who was evidently viewed by his people as a living God. His death at just 19 years old was as unexpected as his ascension to the throne at such a young age. His royal burial is said to be one of the greatest archeological discoveries of all time.

King Tut's predecessor, Akhenaten, threw the country into turmoil by replacing all the gods with just *one god, Aten,* the sun disk. Tut sought to return Egypt's original beliefs. His life may have been short, but that did not matter because, for King Tut, death was nothing more than a mere beginning. He achieved more glory in death than he could ever hope to achieve during his reign in Egypt. Since King Tut was still a young boy when he became king, a lot of his decisions were heavily influenced by his advisors. In particular, he was guided by one advisor named Ay. It was believed that Ay was the main mastermind, hiding in the shadows of the pharaohs before him. Ay even served Tut's father before him, and after the young King Tut died, Ay became the pharaoh, although he only lasted a short while.

During his reign, King Tut rebuilt temples and sought to denounce the legacy that his father left behind. He moved the capital of Egypt back to Thebes. He married his half-sister Ankhesenamun, and they had two daughters who both died in infancy, according to history. King Tut's reign was relatively unremarkable, and he would not have made it into the history books if not for the events that happened thousands of years *after* his death. Arguably, it was these events that landed him the title of the most famous pharaoh in history. Discovered by Howard Carter, he and his daughter became the first people in 3,000 years to enter King Tut's tomb. Almost immediately, Carter realized what a discovery he had made as everywhere in the tomb was laden with gold. Although the discovery was credited as one of the greatest discoveries of all time, it was also a discovery that was plagued by mysterious deaths.

One warning that was discovered went something like this:

Curse to all those who disturb the pharaoh's rest. Those that would break the seal of the tomb will be met with death by diseases no doctor can diagnose".

Eerily, many of the excavators succumbed to strange and inexplicable deaths. Months after the opening of King Tut's tomb, mysterious deaths began plaguing some of the workers involved in the excavation. The newspapers were running rampant with tales of the curse of King Tut's tomb. Lord Carnarvon, the financier behind King Tut's excavation, was one of the many mysterious deaths recorded. He had supposedly scratched open a mosquito bite, which then became infected. He succumbed to the blood infection just 4 months after the tomb was opened. The media ran wild with the story, claiming King Tut had finally claimed revenge on the man who was responsible for disturbing his rest. Strictly speaking, King Tut was not a hero, but the stories of his cursed tomb no doubt make him one of the most infamous pharaohs in history.

Thutmose III

Thutmose III was a clever general who added new lands to ancient Egypt. Under his leadership, Egypt seized Syria to the north and Palestine to the east. He was the first king to ever truly document a battle in specific detail. With his stepmother Hatshepsut, Thutmose III became co-regent for the first 22 years of his reign. When Hatshepsut died, Thutmose III became pharaoh and immediately set his eyes on the Levant region.

As the pharaoh, Thutmose the 3rd was not a general who stood back behind the army and called the shots. He was at the front of the army, in a chariot, leading his men into the heart of the battle. He would make 16 raids in 20 years and conquer much of the Near East, from the Euphrates to Nubia, during 17 known military campaigns. The first campaign began in Year 2 of his independent reign. Known as the Battle of Megiddo, this was the first battle in history that was recorded in relative detail. These military exploits are recorded on the walls of Amun-Ra's Temple at Karnak. They were originally produced on parchment in a journal by Thutmose III's scribe, Thanuny. Attempting to block Thutmose III's expansion into the Levant, the king of Kadesh, Durusha, mustered an army of about 10-15 thousand men and advanced to Megiddo, where they constructed a defense to await the Egyptian army. With about the same number of soldiers, Thutmose III marched to the loyal city of Gaza in 10 days. After a day of rest, he pressed on and reached Yehem. Here, he sent out scouts and had to make a vital decision on how to reach Megiddo. To arrive at the destination, there were several routes they could take. Two of these routes were straightforward, placing the army in the north of the town. The third, however, was through a narrow pass. The officers pointed out that this route was dangerous and left them vulnerable and open to the possibility of being ambushed since it was really only wide enough for a single file.

Thutmose believed that if his generals counseled him to take the easiest route, then his enemies would probably assume that he would travel that way, too. Therefore, Thutmose chose the unexpected route instead and took the narrow pass. He marched at the head of the army with almost total disregard for his own personal safety. Emerging from the mouth of the Wadi, he saw that his enemies had wrongly anticipated his moves. He had, in fact, come out between the north and south wings of their army. The next morning, they attacked, even though King Durusha had the higher ground. This was the ground that was adjacent to the fortress. Meanwhile, the rest of the Egyptian line was positioned in a concave formation. The formation consisted of three wings that exposed both Canaanite flanks.

Thutmose III and his army easily won the battle, taking many prisoners, horses, and chariots for their own.

Thutmose III was also a great builder. He built more than 50 temples during his reign, most of which were in Karnak. He erected two obelisks at Karnak, one of which now stands in the Hippodrome at Istanbul. At the east end of the Karnak complex, he built his Festival Hall, which had a unique design.

Horus, the Falcon God

Known for defeating Seth, Horus is a hero in ancient Egyptian mythology. According to the prophecy, Horus was said to be the one who will bring "light back to Egypt." He was said to be the one who would end the darkness that was caused by Seth and his reign.

Legend has it that Horus accepted a challenge from Seth to determine who should be King. They both transformed themselves into hippos and had a competition to see who could hold their breath underwater the longest. It is said that Horus turned to his mother Isis for an advantage in the challenge, hoping to kill Seth in his moment of weakness. But Isis felt sympathy for her brother Seth, and so she refused. Seth won this first competition.

Horus was so angry at his mother for failing to help him that he cut off her head, carried it up a mountain, and threw it away! Shortly after however, Thoth reunited Isis' head with her body, bringing her back to life.

The battle between Horus and Seth would go on to rage for many months until the Court of Gods finally stepped in and demanded that Horus and Seth reconcile. Seth, being the evil one who was only pretending to be benevolent, asked Horus to attend a feast at his palace. During the night, Seth would attempt to rape his nephew in the hopes of making him unworthy for the throne, but Horus managed to defend himself.

Their battles would continue for many years, with each one trying to prove their worthiness over the other. After 80 years, the judges decided to seek a final verdict. They sought the advice of Osiris, who was now ruling the Underworld. Osiris determined that his son, Horus, was the rightful ruler and that Seth should be kept in chains as a prisoner. Horus took the throne that was rightfully his, and thus began Horus's reign over Egypt. The pharaohs who would go on to reign over Egypt were believed to be his descendants.

The story of Horus is a popular one in ancient Egyptian mythology because he is seen as the hero who avenged his father's death and reclaimed what was rightfully his. His pursuit of the throne was not done only out of power, but out of honor for his father and his family. It was his right to reclaim the throne, and that is one of the reasons Horus was so loved and respected by the Egyptian people.

Chapter 4: The Monsters

Ancient Egypt was truly a remarkable place and time. It was fascinating, from its gods and legendary pharaohs to the mythological monsters that make its history that much more excited. However, the details of ancient Egyptian myths sometimes seem to contradict each other. One text can describe one creature or monster so differently from the next, but what each variant represents is an understanding of how the Egyptians tried to make sense of their world and their gods. Because the Egyptian culture survived for such a long time, these myths morphed over time, resulting in different versions of the same stories. Mythology was a profound element of the culture at the time, being a source of inspiration for many of the religious rituals and beliefs that existed.

Several sources are believed to have influenced the creation and evolution of these myths and creatures, and it always links back to the Egyptians' natural environment and what they were surrounded with. Like the Nile, for example, which was a very important resource to the people at the time. The sun was also an important influence, and thus, the people of Egypt believed that the sun and water were the very symbols and essence of life. However, the sun and the water were also believed to bring destruction at times in the form of floods and famine. In Egyptian mythology, common themes that appear to emerge the most center around chaos, order, and rebirth or renewal. A central component in many of these stories are the mythical creatures the Ancient Egyptians believed in. In this chapter, we'll be taking a look at some of the most famous and revered creatures that featured Egyptian mythology throughout the years.

The Sphinx

Perhaps the best known and most easily recognizable creature even to this very day that is associated with mythology and ancient Egypt is none other than the Sphinx. The reason that we still know about it today is because of the massive statue famously referred to as *The Great Sphinx of Giza*. The Sphinx in ancient Egypt has a very, very long history of being shrouded in secrecy and intrigue. It was viewed by countless cultures in the world as the guardian of knowledge and for their affinity for speaking in riddles. The Sphinx does not have a history of real, living existence, and instead exists only in art, literature, and architecture. It represents the human desire for that which is greater than themselves.

Typically depicted with the head of a human and the body of a lion, the Sphinx is known for being a rather ferocious creature. Depicted as both beautiful and alluring, yet dangerous and deadly at the same time, the Sphinx was the guardian of knowledge and a threat to evil. If you encountered a Sphinx, the outcome could be both destructive and confusing. Ultimately, it was believed by the Egyptians of the time that the Sphinx represented mankind's desire and capacity to penetrate the universe's mysteries, while at the same time serving as a warning that to venture into the unknown could be a risky endeavor.

The ancient Egyptians had three categories of the Sphinx. First was the *Androsphinx,* which had the head of a person and the body of a lion. The second was the *Criosphinx,* with the body of a lion and the head of a ram. The third was the *Hieracosphinx,* with the body of a lion and the head of a hawk. The tale was always such that the Sphinx should be approached with caution, despite being alluring. The most famous attribute of the Sphinx is a talent for riddles. It is said that the Sphinx uses its cunning to concoct these riddles and then use them to test the worthiness of man. According to legend, the Sphinx would attack anyone who failed to answer its riddles correctly.

Bennu

This mythical bird is something the ancient Egyptians believed to be associated with rebirth, creation, and the sun. In fact, the Egyptians believed that the Bennu played a part in the creation of the world. Bennu was given the moniker, *"He who came into being by himself."* There is speculation that the Phoenix, which is popular in Greek mythology, was derived from the Bennu.

Since the Bennu was a symbol that was associated with rebirth, it also became the symbol that was associated with the god, *Osiris*. The story of Bennu is found in the Egyptian Book of the Dead. Based on that account, the Bennu created itself when it burned on a Holy Tree in one of the sacred precincts of *Ra's* temple. Specifically, the Temple of Horus. The Bennu, or versions of it, went by many names in nearly every ancient tradition here on earth. The most common name it went by was Phoenix, which was associated with not only Greek mythology, but Chinese and Phoenician legends too. According to the lore, the Bennu would build a nest of cinnamon twigs when it came to the end of its life cycle. It would then light the nest on fire and burn alongside it. Out of the ashes, a young new Bennu would arise. This is much like the story of the phoenix rising from the ashes.

As the sacred bird of Egypt, it was also believed that the Bennu would escort souls into heaven.

Griffin

This creature was said to be part lion and part eagle, and it has been used by various societies throughout Egyptian history.

Evidence points to the existence of these Griffins in ancient Egyptian art discovered as early as 3000 BC. The Griffin is a creation that is depicted with the head, talons, and the wings of a great bird, but with the tail and hindquarters belonging to a lion. There is something universally fearsome about this mythological creature.

The Griffin is a legendary creature that has been used in modern times in books and movies. However, its origins stretch as far back as ancient Greece, Persia, and of course, ancient Egypt. The Eagle is believed to be the king of the birds while the mighty lion is the king of the beasts. Combining the most powerful elements of land and sky, the Griffin was considered an extremely powerful and majestic creature. Griffins were thought to be very wise and were often shown guarding the gold and treasure of Kings. Some legends suggest that the Griffin was more of a trickster, much like the Sphinx, who would challenge people to solve its riddles. The winners would be allowed to keep the treasure and their lives. The losers would not.

The Sphinx is similar to the Griffin in appearance with the body of a lion but the head of a human. Some historians believe that the idea of the Griffin came from dinosaur remains found from the Cretaceous period. The Griffin was commonly used to represent wisdom and power. Because many mythological creatures in these ancient societies tended to overlap, the

Griffin was also found in Greek mythology, where it is said to have pulled the chariot of Apollo, the god of the Sun (in Greek myth). Apollo would have to travel from the Sun to the earth, meaning he needed a creature that could fly, making the Griffin the perfect choice.

Abtu

The ancient Egyptians believed at some point that Isis transformed into a sacred fish. The fish's name was Abtu. Not much is known about what Abtu actually looked like since there are seemingly no visual representations remaining of the creature. The only evidence of its existence was the discovery of a hymn of passage that was dedicated to *Ra* himself. This is in a passage from *A Hymn of Praise to Ra When He Riseth In the Eastern Part of Heaven*. The passage was translated in 1984 by Robert Guisepi, and it simply reads: *"Let me behold the Abtu Fish at this season."*

Uraeus

Uraeus, the Egyptian snake or cobra, was used as a symbol of royalty, divine authority, deity, and sovereignty in ancient Egypt. Unlike a lot of the other mythological creatures in Egypt, this revered deity refers to the symbol of a rearing cobra, which, in Egyptian mythology, represented the divine authority of

Egypt's pharaohs. The symbol is found all over the place in ancient relics. Uraeus is often associated with the Wadjet, a goddess who was one of the earliest Egyptian deities.

Uraeus is a name that quite literally means *"rearing cobra."* As one of the earliest deities of Kemet, the Uraeus symbol served two purposes. One, since most pharaohs came from Upper Kemet, it symbolized the King's rule over lower Kemet. Two, it was also a symbol of protection for the king and his royal representations. It was believed that the Uraeus would spit fire at his enemies. During the first intermediate period, the Kemet was divided and fell into anarchy. After many years of uncertainty in Upper and Lower Kemet, a king in the south finally managed to reunite the entire country. Following this, the cobra statue began to appear next to the vulture in hieroglyphics. The vulture was a symbol of Nekhbet, who was the goddess of Upper Kemet. Together, the two symbols were known as *Nebet Tawy,* which translates to mean *"the two ladies."*

This led to the creation of a new title for Kemet's rulers. Some rulers of Kemet wore two cobras on their headdress. The cobras represented two kingdoms, which were Kush and Kemet. Many male rulers of the 25th dynasty can be found with this symbol above their brows. In ancient Kemet, women of royalty were also recognized, but unlike the men, they had a single cobra above their brows. Some royal women had both the vulture *and* the cobra adorning their headdress. This meant that they had been elevated to the rank of *goddess* among the queens. This was a tradition that started among the women of the 18th dynasty.

Apophis

In every good mythological story, there's always a villain, an entity that threatens chaos and destruction, the end of everything we know. When we take a look at Egyptian mythology, that evil takes the form of Apophis (also referred to as Apep), the god of chaos, darkness, and destruction. In some of the earliest stories, Apophis was once the God of the Sun. He was later cast aside by Ra. Having been dethroned, Apophis harbored a great deal of resentment towards the Gods, and he vowed to make it as difficult as possible for Ra to succeed in his task of bringing the dawn every day. In some versions of events, Apophis was born from darkness and chaos, making him the mortal enemy of light, fueling his desire to overthrow the balance of all things. Apophis takes the form of an enormous serpent, as large as 50-feet long, which is why he has the nicknames 'evil lizard' and 'serpent from the Nile'.

The word Apep is derived from the Egyptian word meaning "slither" and could also be used as a term for being "spat out," which would refer to the way Apophis was shunned and removed from his position as God of the Sun. There are even some depictions of Apophis being described as a crocodile that swims in the dark waters of the underworld. In later Greek and Roman stories, he was described as an enormous golden snake, several miles long with a head of stone. Apophis was just one of the many gods to have been born from the goddess *Neith*, making him brother to many of the predominant gods in Egypt, including Ra and Sobek. As the legend goes, every day, when Ra would travel across the sky in his solar barge, he would bring the dawn with him, and Apophis would await to attack the Sun God so he could one day successfully plunge the world into deep darkness. Thus, Ra sought the help of several defenders to make the journey with him.

When Apophis would show up to block the way, they would slit the belly of the serpent open, allowing Ra to pass. There is a story regarding the two where one morning, Ra was performing his duties when Apophis swallowed his barge whole. Ra transformed himself into a cat, and with the help of Seth, they were able to cut themselves free from inside Apophis and continue their journey.

In other stories, Apophis would hypnotize Ra and all of his followers. Only the god, Seth, would be able to resist the serpent, and he would repel him with his great spear. Despite being defeated every day, Apophis continued to swallow the Sun God and his followers, knowing that if they were unable to escape just once, he would succeed and plunge the world into darkness.

Despite being considered a god, Apophis was rarely worshipped by anyone. There was even a book solely dedicated to stopping the serpent God, which included a collection of rituals meant to keep him at bay. The people of Egypt believed that Apophis would lead an army of demons that would prey upon the living and the dead each year. In order to stop this, the priests of Ra's temple would conduct an annual ritual known as the *Banishing of Apep*. An effigy of the serpent god was taken into the temple and imbued of all the evil of the land; the effigy was then beaten, cursed, and burnt to keep Apophis away and help the gods ensure that the Sun would rise again the next day. The book containing the rituals and magic spells devoted to stopping him was known as *The Book of Apophis*.

Ammit

Ammit was the "devourer of souls." According to Egyptian mythology, when a person died, before they could enter the afterlife, they would have to have their heart weighed against the feather on a scale. If the scale was balanced, then they were allowed to pass on freely. If their heart weighed heavy, they were deemed unworthy of entry. Their soul was devoured by Ammit, and they would suffer a second death with no chance of a peaceful afterlife. Ammit was sometimes depicted as a goddess of the underworld, but she was never really worshipped, though her image was thought to ward off evil. She was most commonly referred to as a demon, a malevolent supernatural being.

Her name roughly translates to *"devourer of souls"* or *"devourer of the dead."* Ammit had the head of a crocodile, the torso of a lioness or leopard, and the lower body and hind legs of a hippopotamus. This may sound like a strange mixture of animals, but these were the most ferocious and terrifying creatures known to the ancient Egyptians. The Book of the Dead referred to Ammit as The Punisher and Executioner, and she was often believed to be the personification of divine retribution and justice. Ammit would wait in the judgment hall of Two Truths during the weighing of the heart ceremony. Those who were deemed not fit enough to enter the afterlife were given one last chance to explain their life in front of Osiris and his deity judges. If they were still judged to have led a sinful life, then their soul would be given to Ammit.

There are some variations of Ammit where she did not devour the souls of the sinful at all. Instead, the souls who were deemed unworthy of the afterlife were thrown into the Lake of Fire. She was believed to live nearby and acted as the guardian of the Lake of Fire. Although Ammit is rarely depicted as a goddess and more commonly is seen as a demon who devours souls, she is in no way inherently evil. She acts to ensure the order is enforced and is used to ward off evil. She represents the fact that every person is given a chance to defend their actions before final judgment.

Sobek – A Different Tale

Sobek was mentioned briefly in Chapter 2 as one of the Egyptian gods of the water. But there is another side to Sobek that the Egyptians believed in. A more fearsome, gruesome side, as legend would have it.

Creator of the River Nile, Sobek was both revered and feared at the same time. He was aggressive and unpredictable, yet some still called him a gift-bringer and even a protector. Sobek is the ancient Egyptian crocodile god of the Nile. His appearance is what makes him so easy to identify, but even that itself slightly varies. Sometimes he was shown as a large crocodile similar to those found in the River Nile, and other times, he appears a human man with the head of a crocodile. It was Sobek's appearance that made him so terrifying. Crocodiles were just one of the many species of animals found in the Nile that were capable of devouring a man.

Over the years, there have been numerous tales attempting to explain to us how the Nile was formed. In some of these stories, the river was created from the sweat that poured from Sobek's body. Being able to rule over the River Nile with all of its dangerous and aggressive creatures was no easy task, but because Sobek was able to do this, he was seen as even more dangerous than the creatures themselves. The Nile did also bring with it many positive aspects, like the fact that it provided fertile soil and a means to grow vegetation, essentially giving birth to new life. Sobek was considered to control these waters; he was seen as a fearless protector of the Nile, which often led him to also be an associate of fertility as well as crocodiles in the Nile itself.

Sobek was worshipped by the ancient Egyptian people because of the gifts he gave them. The gifts of vegetation and fertility came from the Nile, but despite this, he was still extremely feared by the people. His reptilian appearance and being the ruler of an environment as harsh as the Nile meant that Sobek was quite often seen as aggressive and unpredictable. His behavior was often attributed to animal instinct, and along with this instinct and his association with fertility, he was regarded as very sexual and very similar to an animal that is unable to control its urges.

Throughout the years, Sobek has been referred to by many names, including *Soket* and *Sukkos,* in ancient Greece. Sobek as we've come to know him today, was first mentioned in the Pyramid Texts of the old kingdom, which are widely regarded as some of the oldest texts to exist. When Sobek first made an appearance, it was in the ancient Egyptian city of Shedet. The ancient Greeks referred to this city as *Crocodylus,* essentially meaning city of the crocodile or crocodile city. As one would expect in the city of the crocodile, Sobek had quite a cult following. There was a large temple built in his name to honor him. The temple was home to a crocodile that people called the *Son of Sobek*. The crocodile was worshipped as the manifestation of the god himself. It was even adorned with gifts of gems, jewelry, and gold. The crocodile was fed and looked after much better than most people in the city, with a diet consisting of luxuries such as meat, wine, and milk with honey. When the crocodile died, much like the Pharaohs of Egypt, it was mummified and then replaced by another crocodile who assumed the role of the *Son of Sobek*. When observing what took place in the city itself, there were numerous Greek historians who recorded that anyone who was killed by a crocodile considered to be the *Son of Sobek* were believed to be divine. The victims would be embalmed and buried in a sacred coffin, and special funeral rites would be performed by the priests of the Nile. Some of the ancient Egyptians kept crocodiles just like house pets, believing that feeding a crocodile would mean they would receive Sobek's blessing. Despite Sobek being worshipped in the old kingdom, it wasn't until the Middle Kingdom when the influence of Sobek really began to grow.

During this period, he was often associated with Horus, and there are even numerous depictions of the two gods fused together with the head of a falcon placed on the body of a crocodile. It was also believed that Horus might have taken the form of a crocodile when attempting to retrieve the body parts of Osiris that Seth had scattered around the rivers of Egypt. There is a story where the four sons of Horus were drowning in the River Nile, but Sobek appeared and gathered them all up in a giant net, placing the children back on land. In another story, when Seth killed his brother Osiris, he disembodied him and threw his body parts in the rivers of Egypt. One morning, Sobek saw the parts of Osiris in the Nile, and they looked so appetizing to Sobek that he could not resist and began to eat the parts of Osiris as they floated by. Sobek was eventually punished for defiling the god in this manner by having his tongue removed, which is why when we see crocodiles in Egyptian mythology, they are rarely ever depicted as having tongues. Some stories depict Sobek as showing compassion to his fellow gods, and in others, he completely disregards them. As you can see, these stories morphed over centuries to fit the beliefs of the people at the time.

Sobek is constantly described as being very instinctual and almost primitive. By the time of the New Kingdom, Sobek's depiction once again changed. Rather than being shown as fused together with Horus, he was more commonly associated with Ra himself, and once again, the two gods were shown as being one entity, creating the new God known as *Sobek-Ra*. Sobek's parents were quite powerful, influential gods in Egyptian mythology. Neith, the ancient goddess of war, was his mother while his father was Seth, the god of storms and chaos. Some scholars would argue that Sobek's father could have been a host of other gods. His close association with the god Horus has led many to believe that he may have played a role in Sobek's creation. A theory that is not quite as common is that his father was Khnum, the god of the source of the Nile and one of the oldest Egyptian deities, known for his depiction as a man with the head of a ram. Khnum was considered the original source and God of the River Nile, a connection that he would share with Sobek.

Sobek's wife was Renenutet, goddess of snakes and often considered a protector of the harvest. Despite Sobek being associated with a number of other gods that he could be considered father to, there are no definitive theories about this. Nonetheless, he was extremely valued as the protector of the Nile, a resource that many depended on to survive. Sobek being a crocodile, one of the deadliest predators in Egypt, meant he was immensely feared, but at the same time, he was also respected and revered, with cities and temples built in his honor. There were a number of crocodiles found mummified in tombs and pyramids that show us they were treated in almost the same manner as the great pharaohs of Egypt.

Some tales depict Sobek as once being a dark God, mostly because of his association with Seth and crocodiles. Sobek became somewhat symbolic to the pharaohs of Egypt, and Sobek's great strength and power were thought to represent the Pharaoh's own power. They even looked towards Sobek in times of need, believing that he would give pharaohs and their armies the strength and fortitude to overcome all obstacles, as well as protect them from evil magic. Despite Sobek's unpredictable and aggressive nature, he was never really considered evil. He was almost seen as a force of nature, uncontrollable, instinctual, and unyielding in his role.

Chapter 5: Famous Egyptian Mythology Stories

The Story of Ra and the Sun Boat

In Egyptian mythology, Ra is infamously known as the Sun God. Once the greatest of all gods, time eventually wore him down, and when he became too old to continue his duties, Ra decided that it was time for him to relinquish his power and make his way to the skies above. As the god of the sun, one of Ra's many duties was to drive away the darkness each day. To do this, Ra had to cross the skies each day in his sun boat. When twilight came, Ra and his sun boat would plunge into the waters of the sea, heading towards the underworld.

In the underworld, Ra would have to sail through the darkness and make his way across the 12 gates. The 12 gates of the underworld were the 12 gates to the nether world. To go through each gate would take Ra and his sun boat an hour. At one of those gates, Osiris, the lord of the underworld was waiting. Before Ra would leave the underworld, the terrible serpent Apophis would attack. Apophis, a force of chaos, would attempt to destroy Ra and his vessel. Each day it would seem that the fearsome serpent was growing closer to accomplishing its goal. One day, Apophis managed to swallow Ra and his sun boat, which put an end to the sunlight in ancient Egypt in the morning. However, Apophis could not contain Ra within her belly and eventually regurgitated him. This event came to be marked as the solar eclipse. Destroying Ra's sun boat became increasingly more difficult after Seth was condemned to navigate the skies with Ra. Seth would help Ra defend his vessel against Apophis, and he would be successful at defeating the destructive serpent several times.

Isis and Osiris - A Tale of True Love

The story of Isis and Osiris is one of the most beautiful love stories of all time. Their tale shows that true love conquers all, even death. Osiris was the king of Egypt, and Isis was his queen, beloved by all the people. They taught men how to honor the gods and live prosperously by growing crops. Isis and Osiris also gave the people laws to live by. However, their brother Seth was jealous of Osiris and plotted against him.

Isis did not trust Seth and was wary of his ways. Whenever her husband would travel around the Kingdom of Egypt, Isis would always be on her guard, watching over her King. One day, Osiris held a large banquet for his court, and Seth was also invited, despite Isis' wishes. Seth boasted to Osiris of a wonderful coffin he had been given, a coffin made of the finest wood, gilded and painted. Eventually, Osiris' curiosity got the better of him, and he asked Seth to bring this coffin in for all to see. When the coffin was delivered, Seth promised that he would give the coffin to anyone who would fit into it. Many tried to fit into the coffin, but none were able because unbeknownst to Osiris, Seth had taken his measurements and had the coffin made especially for him.

After many tried and failed, Osiris decided that he would try, but once he lay in the coffin, Seth and his accomplices quickly nailed the lid shut, trapping Osiris alive inside it. Seth's guard held the people of Egypt back as the coffin was thrown into the Nile and washed away with the current.

Isis was in despair. She cut off a length of her hair and dressed in clothes of mourning as she set out in search of her husband. Isis wandered everywhere until one day she heard some children say that they had seen a coffin floating in the Nile. Isis entered the land of Byblos, where she heard rumors of a tree beginning to grow on the Nile's shores. The locals told Isis that the coffin had floated ashore and gotten stuck in a bush. Because of Osiris's divine essence, the bush grew and blossomed into a large tree that was later cut down by the then King of Byblos, and the wood was used to build his palace.

Isis ventured to the palace with the help of the villagers and waited outside the palace for the Queen's maidens. She told the maidens she was an Egyptian hairdresser and plaited their hair while quietly breathing a divine scent around them.

The maidens brought Isis to the queen. The queen took a liking to Isis and asked her to take care of the young prince. Time passed, and Isis spent her days in the palace until she finally found the tree trunk that enclosed her husband's coffin. Each night while the young prince was asleep, Isis would venture to the room where the coffin was and weep over her husband's body. More time passed, and Isis eventually grew fond of the young prince and decided that she would make him immortal.

One night while the prince slept, Isis carried him to the pillar where the coffin was hidden and lit a fire. She lowered the sleeping prince into the flames and began to chant her magic incantation. As the fire consumed the young prince's mortality, Isis transformed into a swallow, mourning the way she did every night. The queen, who was sleeping nearby, awoke to the sound of the flames. She rushed to the room and cried out in horror at what she saw before her. Isis transformed into her original form, and the magical fire died out. Isis revealed her true identity to the queen and requested that the queen give her the pillar with the coffin of her husband. Once the coffin was removed, she drenched the pieces of the wood in oil, wrapped them in linen, and asked the Queen to keep the pieces in the Byblos temple.

Isis traveled by boat on the Nile, heading for Egypt with the coffin beside her. While traveling, she opened the coffin and looked upon Osiris. Osiris looked as if he was sleeping, and Isis embraced her husband's body. She continued to make her way through the marshlands to bury her husband, which would allow him to move onto the afterlife. But one night while they were out hunting, Seth and his men came across the gold coffin. Afraid of being punished for his treachery, Seth ordered his men to help him rip Osiris's body into pieces and spread his parts all over the land of Egypt. When Isis saw the empty casket, her anguished cries would shake the entire Heavens and the Earth. Isis sought help from her sister Nephthys, who came to console her, and together they traveled all across Egypt to recover Osiris's body parts. Isis and Nephthys spent many long and sorrowful years searching throughout the land of Egypt, but Isis never gave up. Each time they found a piece of Osiris's body, they erected an altar to the gods as a way of giving thanks. Finally, Isis recovered every missing piece of Osiris's body, and she made him Egypt's first mummy.

Drawing on every ounce of magic she had, Isis breathed life into Osiris once more and, in doing so, they conceived an heir that would one day grow up to challenge Seth. Osiris went on to become known as the King of the Land of the Dead. The lovers were eventually reunited, this time for all eternity.

The Story of Isis and The Seven Scorpions

From a swamp emerged a woman in rags, and by her side were seven scorpions. These giant scorpions walked steadily by the woman's side, accompanying her as she carried a little baby in her arms and headed for the nearest village where she intended to beg for food. As the woman approached a magnificent mansion, the woman of the house immediately shut the door, slamming it in her face because she was disgusted by her grimy clothes and found the woman's unusual companions strange. The woman walked away and continued her journey down the path until she arrived at another cottage. The woman of the cottage felt sorry for the woman and her child, and invited the woman into her home, offering her whatever she had. This happened to be nothing more than a simple meal and a bed that was made out of straw.

Little did the woman of the cottage know that her guest was not who she believed her to be. This was no ordinary beggar. The woman was Isis, the most powerful goddess in ancient Egypt, and Isis was traveling in disguise because she was trying to hide from her brother Seth. Seth had just murdered her husband Osiris and he now wanted to murder Isis's infant son. The infant was none other than Horus, the child who would one day grow up to defeat Seth and avenge his father's death. To escape her brother and avoid being caught, Isis had to be very careful and travel in a disguise that would make her almost unrecognizable. Although she could not risk using her powers, she was not without help. The goddess of venomous creatures, Serqet, had sent seven of her fiercest servants, the scorpions who were traveling with Isis, to guard and protect Isis and Horus.

As Isis and Horus made themselves at home in the humble woman's cottage, the scorpions were angry at the rich woman for daring to insult their divine mistress. Each of the scorpions combined their venom and gave it to one of the seven, a scorpion named Tefen. Tefen would wait until the dead of night before he ventured to the rich woman's mansion. Crawling under the door and entering the mansion, Tefen saw the rich woman's young son. The son was sleeping peacefully at the time, and Tefen gave the son a mighty sting. Isis and the humble woman in the cottage were awakened by the sound of the rich woman's loud wailing. Looking out the window of the cottage, Isis saw a mother running out into the street, weeping uncontrollably, as she cradled her son in her arms. Isis recognized the woman as the one who had turned her away, and when she saw the scene before her, she knew what her scorpions had done. Isis took the rich woman's son and cradled him in her arms as she recited a powerful spell, calling Tefen's poison out from the body of the son. Isis recited the spell with the name of the seven scorpions, and with each name that she called out, the poison of the scorpion was neutralized.

The rich woman was so grateful that she wept at how callous she had been toward Isis. The rich woman offered Isis all her wealth as repentance for her behavior. The humble woman of the cottage watched everything that happened before her in awe, realizing that she had, in fact, invited none other than the goddess Isis into her home.

A Tale of Isis and The Name of the Sun God

Isis was an ingenious woman, smarter than many of the gods who existed during the time. She knew everything that went on in heaven and on earth. It was her desire that she and Horus be positioned in the pantheon of Gods. She knew that if she were to accomplish her goal, she had to find out Ra's secret name. Knowing Ra's true name brought with it an incomparable power. One day, Isis discovered Ra asleep with a long dribble of saliva hanging from the corner of this mouth. As she watched, the saliva grew heavier until it was so heavy it finally fell on the ground. Isis immediately gathered it and mixed it with clay, creating a very poisonous snake in the process. Once she was finished, she took the final step and breathed life into the serpent. Isis had been watching Ra for weeks, and she knew his every movement. She knew that he often left the palace for his walks, and on his route, he would always pass a crossroads.

It was here that Isis would leave her snake to do its damage. When Ra was walking along his usual path, Isis's snake bit him. The god saw and felt nothing, but he soon felt the poison as it coursed through his veins. In pain and anguish, Ra called out to the other gods for help. It wasn't long before Ra was sweating and shivering, but the other gods were helpless and could do nothing to save their beloved leader. Isis then made her dramatic entrance and told Ra she could heal him, but in return, she wanted his name. Of course, Ra refused. Isis extended her offer again, but once more, the Sun God declined. Only when his pain became too great to bear did Ra finally acquiesce, but he made Isis promise that she would never real this secret to anyone except for her son Horus. Isis agreed and at once spoke words of magic, expelling the poison from Ra's body. Ra was cured, and Isis and Horus got what they wanted all along.

A Tale of Thoth and The Eye of Horus

When he was born, Horus already knew that his father was murdered by his uncle Seth. He knew that it was his fate to bring about divine vengeance for his father. From the time he was young, Horus was dutiful in all his efforts to one day bring his uncle to justice, and in doing so, he would restore order to the world. The mighty battle between Seth and Horus was an epic one, a battle that would go on to last for many decades. At one stage of his battle, Horus was on the verge of killing Seth with the help of his mother until Isis had a sudden change of heart. Her mercy saved Seth, and Horus was so enraged at this turn of events that he turned on his mother and attacked her so viciously that he incited the anger of the other gods. He swung wildly with his copper knife, and he managed to sever her head. Luckily, Thoth was quickly able to repair the damage and bring Isis back to life.

Horus was ashamed of what he had done, and he fled into the wilderness while the gods searched the earth for him. Eventually, Seth found him resting beside an oasis. Seth transformed into a black boar to launch his attack, and before Horus knew what was happening, Seth had gouged out his left eye and tossed it beyond the edge of the world. Horus got revenge by ripping off Seth's testicles. Since it was a battle between two gods, the injuries had cosmic connotations. Horus's was the moon whose light was thereby lost to the world, and Seth's partial emasculation was afterward used to explain the infertility of the desert. Meanwhile, with the moon gone, the earth was plunged into the deepest darkness. With disaster on the horizon, it was Thoth who would come to the rescue. He was the peacemaker during the conflict between the two gods, and he now searched beyond the world's confines high and low until he discovered the missing eye. Thoth pieced it together and restored it to Horus, and, in doing so, he brought back the light to the night sky. The Eye of Horus was afterward represented by the Wadjet amulet, which is a protective symbol against all forms of evil.

A Tale of Bastet's Festival

Daughter of the sun god Ra, the feline deity Bastet was widely venerated throughout ancient Egypt. By the late period, Bastet's festival was one of the most popular in the ritual calendar. For ceremonial purposes, the town of Bubastis, 50 miles northeast of modern Cairo, was best approached by water. The ancient Greek historian Herodotus wrote that they came in barges for the festival. When they arrived at Bubastis, they rejoiced and were merry at the festival. There were elaborate sacrifices, and more wine was consumed during the festival than during all the rest of the year. People arrived by the thousands to pay their respects at the red granite temple erected in honor of the goddess. Cats that have died are taken to Bubastis where they are embalmed and buried in sacred receptacles. Thousands of the dead creatures were mummified and interred in underground galleries there and at other sites so that they might carry their owners' messages more swiftly to the realm of the gods. In the main temple of Bubastis, the catacombs of mummified cats and several pharaonic shrines prove that even the highest born in Egypt, the pharaohs and those of royal blood, worshipped the mighty goddess.

A Tale of Mankind's Destruction

Ra, as a ruler of men, was past his prime, but his age did not prevent him from hearing that men were mocking him and plotting to overthrow him. Ra called for a secret conference among the gods, where he sought their advice. Nun was the one whom he listened to the most, since Nun was the oldest. Nun advised Ra to punish the blasphemers by burning them with his blazing heat. Ra did this, but his victims escaped by running for shelter. Thus, Ra reconvened with the gods who then suggested that he send the goddess Hathor to punish humankind.

In the guise of the lioness Sekmet, Hathor perpetrated a savage slaughter. By the time she was called by Ra to return home, she had developed a ravenous taste for blood and was single-minded about returning to Earth to destroy the rest of mankind. Ra was distressed since he meant only to teach people a lesson, not to wipe them out. While Hathor rested, he sent messengers to Aslan to bring back a consignment of red ochre. He ordered the high priests of Heliopolis to pound it while the servant girls brew barley beer. The mixing of the two elements produced seven thousand jugs of an intoxicating drink that looked like blood. Ra asked for the jugs to be emptied over the fields where Hathor had planned her destruction. The next day, Hathor was flying over the fields when she saw a lot of blood and swooped down for a drink. She consumed too much and fell into a stupor. On regaining her senses, she had forgotten her original aim and set off home again. As a reconciliatory gesture, Ra decreed that the Egyptian people could drink as much as they liked at Hathor's festivals.

Anpu and Bata - A Tale of Two Brothers

Once upon a time, there were two brothers. Anpu was the older brother, and Bata was the younger brother. When their parents died, Anpu was already married with a house of his own. Anpu took his little brother with him after the death of his parents and treated him like a son. He welcomed Bata and told him to treat his home as his own. As Bata grew up, he became a great farmer, and no man could compare to his quality of work. No one could equal his skills in the whole land. Because Anpu loved his brother so much, his wife became very jealous, and she wanted to destroy their relationship.

One day, while Anpu and Bata were in the fields, they needed some seeds. So Anpu sent Bata home to retrieve them. Bata found Anpu's wife combing her hair when he arrived. He asked the wife to move aside so he could quickly get the seeds and returned to Anpu, who was waiting in the field. As the wife watched Bata measuring and carrying the containers, she admired how strong and handsome he was. She tried to stroke his arm, but Bata turned her away, telling her that he would never betray his brother. The wife was furious at being rejected by Bata, so she tore her own clothes and rubbed grease on her legs to make it look like she had been attacked.

Later, Anpu returned to find his wife crying, and his wife told him that Bata had attacked her after she pushed him away for trying to kiss her. She begged an angry Anpu to kill his brother for dishonoring her. A furious Anpu waited with a sharpened spear for the sun to go down and for Bata to return so he could kill his brother. Bata, fearing for his life, began to run. Anpu pursued him, his anger giving him speed and strength. Desperate, Bata cried out to Ra and begged him to save him from his brother's wrath. Ra heard his plea and created a river between the two brothers that flowed wide and deep. In the river were hungry crocodiles, and Anpu was afraid of crossing the river.

Bata called out to his brother from across the river and asked why Anpu would try to kill him without giving him a chance to explain. Bata swore on Ra that he never tried to seduce Anpu's wife, and that it was all a lie. To prove himself, he took a reed knife and wounded himself. When Anpu saw what his brother did, he realized that his wife had lied. Bata collapsed on the ground, weak from the loss of blood. Anpu was desperate to help him, but he could not cross the river. Bata told Anpu that they must part for now and that he would go toward the Valley of Cedars. He told his brother that he would put his heart at the top of the cedar tree's blossom, and if one day it is cut down,

Anpu will be able to find it and bring him back to life again. He tells Anpu that if he one day receives a jar with beer that froths, it is a sign that he should seek out his brother.

Anpu agrees, and when he returns home, he kills his wife for her deception. Bata continued on to the Valley of Cedars, placing his heart at the top of the cedar tree. In the Valley of Cedars, he meets Ennead, one of the Egyptian deities. Ennead takes pity on Bata. Khnum helps to create a wife for Bata, but because she is created by the divine, she is sought after by the pharaoh. The pharaoh orders his men to cut down the tree containing Bata's heart, and Bata dies.

Shortly after, Anpu received a jar where the beer was frothy. He recognized the sign and knew that it was time for him to make his journey to the Valley of Cedars. Anpu spent three years searching for the heart of his brother, and when he finally found it, he placed Bata's heart in a bowl of cold water. As promised, Bata was then resurrected. Taking the form of a bull, Bata went to see his wife who was now living with the pharaoh. The wife recognized Bata and asked the pharaoh if she can eat the bull's liver. When the bull is sacrificed, two drops of blood fall, and from that spot, two Persea trees begin to grow.

Bata then took on the form of a tree and addressed his wife. She then asked the pharaoh to chop the Persea trees and use the wood from these trees to make furniture. In doing so, a splinter from the tree ends up in her mouth, and she becomes pregnant, eventually giving birth to a son who would one day become the crown prince. Little did she know that the crown prince was none other than Bata, once again resurrected. When the prince became the king, he appointed Anpu as the crown prince. The two brothers have a happy ending, making peace with each other as they rule the land.

Chapter 6: The Book of Thoth and The Book of the Dead

In ancient Egypt 5,000 years ago or so, just before the rise of Egypt's great pharaohs, hieroglyphics, or pictographs were invented, Egyptians used the occult to document their history and religion, and practiced complex systems of astronomy, astrology, and geometry. They believed their powerful knowledge came from the god Thoth, whom they believed was the Egyptian god of magic. More than just a god of magic, he was the god of writing, astronomy, mathematics, and science. He invented both language and writing. Only priests with special training were allowed access to Thoth's sacred knowledge. Imhotep, the builder of the first pyramid, was one of the chosen ones allowed to access this knowledge. Among the historians who studied the ancient world, some believed he was a person who was later deified through his accomplishments. Others felt this was a mythical entity from the beginning. Legends say that a book of magic written by Thoth contained the secrets of the gods.

The Book of Thoth

The Book of Thoth was considered to exist in the astral plane, and wasn't a physical thing, but something that you had to actually travel in consciousness to arrive at. An individual would get into a special state of mind to contact the Thoth energy wherever it was to be found. It is said that the pyramid or the Sphinx contained the teachings that are found in the pages within the book of Thoth. This means that all measurements, words, and concepts are part of the book of Thoth. But no Book of Thoth has ever been found. The god is said to have buried it beneath the Nile and protected its secrets with a deadly curse. Modern archaeologists eventually discovered that the Babylonians had created much of the knowledge Egyptians credited to Thoth. As early as 4000 BC, they were the first to measure planetary movements. They invented the abacus, the first sequential numeric system, and some of the earliest forms of astrology and astronomy. This information spread to Egypt and helped launch one of history's greatest sculptures, and like the Egyptians, the Babylonians considered their knowledge divine. Every temple became an observatory. They morphed into astronomical observation sites for watching the planets.

The rituals and ceremonies of ancient Egypt were designed to contact the gods. The Egyptians used rituals, incantations, and symbols. The pharaoh was the head of the religion, which meant that the pharaoh was a chief practitioner of both religion and their magic. Much of what is called ceremonial magic, the casting of spells, the use of magic words and incantations, came from the Egyptians. It is said that the Book of Thoth would allow those who knew how to read it to speak to all the animals on earth. They could possess the power of the gods. Those who knew the contents of the book could obtain the means to decipher the ancient secrets and master the earth, the sea, the air, and celestial bodies. It is believed that The Book of Thoth is a book that has all the answers to every question in the universe. It is the key to understanding higher knowledge, according to historical records.

This magical book appeared in Egyptian works of fiction and a wide range of diverse papyrus recordings that have been found spread across the region. The first time that The Book of Thoth was cited was in the Taurus papyrus. That description speaks of a failed attempt at killing a pharaoh by trying to use spells that were taken from the book. Since then, the book was hidden from the rest of the world because the Egyptians believed that the book's overwhelming power had to be protected and stopped from falling into the wrong hands.

There is an ancient text that describes where the book might be found, and the text says this:

"The book will be found at Koptos, in the middle of the river in an iron box. In that iron box is a bronze box, and within that bronze, the box is a wood box. Within that wood box, is a box of ivory and ebony, and within that a silver box. In that silver box lies a gold box, and in that gold box, is the Book of Thoth. Around that great iron box are snakes, scorpions, and all manner of crawling things. Above all, there is a snake that no man can kill. These are what guards the Book of Thoth".

There are legends of those who have attempted to claim the book. An Egyptian prince called Neferkaptah was the one who ultimately succeeded in recovering the book, but the young prince had a terrible price to pay. Neferkaptah cared about the wisdom that was to be gained from the Ancients. He cared about the magic that could be learned from the temple walls, and the magic carved in the pyramids and tombs of kings and priests who died long ago. One day, while the prince was pouring over the carvings on the walls within one of the many ancient shrines, he heard the laughter of a priest who taunted him. The priest told him that everything he was reading was worthless, for only the priest could tell him where the Book of Thoth was. The priest went on to tell him that the book was written by the god of wisdom himself, and upon reading the first page, the reader would be granted the power to enchant the earth and the heavens, mountains, sea, and the abyss. It was only through the book that Neferkaptah would ever come to understand what the birds, beasts, and reptiles said. The priest then told Neferkaptah that upon reading the second page of the book, the prince's eyes would be opened to the secrets of the Egyptian gods themselves. Neferkaptah, desperate for the Book of Thoth, asked the priest to name his terms, promising he would fulfill them. The priest answered, *"First, give me a hundred bars of silver for my funeral, and when I die, I shall be buried like that of a great king."*

Neferkaptah did all that the priest asked, and when the priest had disclosed the information, Neferkaptah hurried home to tell his father, the pharaoh, all that he had learned. The pharaoh asked Neferkaptah what it was that he desired, and Neferkaptah replied that he wanted to sail toward Koptos to claim the book without further delay. Neferkaptah then sailed up the Nile until he arrived at Koptos.

On the fifth day in Koptos, Neferkaptah cast an enchantment as instructed by the priest. With his first spell, he created a small cabin, and in that cabin were men and cattle. With the second spell, he breathed life into his creations and commanded it to sink to the bottom of the river. The cabin sank to the bottom of the Nile, and the men he created began to work in search of the book. The prince then worked on filling one of the royal boats with sand before he cast it out into the middle of the Nile. The boat came to rest on the waters above where the cabin lay down below. They continued slowly sailing along the Nile, as the enchanted men worked below.

Three days after the enchantment, they arrived at the location where the book was supposed to be. Neferkaptah cast a spell and summoned the book from beneath the waters until it rose to the river's surface. The serpent that couldn't be killed was wound around the box tightly, and along and around the box were the snakes and scorpions. Once more, the priest uttered magic and in doing so, immobilized the snakes and the scorpions. They couldn't move, and the prince moved freely and swiftly, unharmed, toward the box until he reached the serpent.

The prince drew his sword and charged toward the snake. In a single blow, he struck off the serpent's head. Immediately, the head and body of the serpent sprang together to reunite, and again, the prince cut off its head. This time, the prince threw the serpent's head into the river. Alas, the head and body of the serpent, reunited once more. Neferkaptah realized it would take cunning and deception to overcome the serpent, so this time, he struck off its head but immediately spread sand on each body part so the serpent could not be whole again. Neferkaptah then made his way to the box to finally retrieve the Book of Thoth. He immediately flung the book open, and his eyes devoured the first page. As the priest prophesized, the prince now had power over the earth and the heavens, the abyss, and the seas, and he knew the language of the birds and the beasts. As he read the second page, he learned the secrets of the sky, sun, moon, and the stars. Neferkaptah then made his way home, but there was a price to be paid.

Upon his return, the gods killed his entire family and tormented the young prince for his actions until the prince could no longer bear it and committed suicide to escape the torment. As a final punishment from the gods, the Book of Thoth was said to be entombed with the young prince, thereby enslaving the ghost of the prince that he shall be the protector of the book for the rest of time. Yet, the allure of the book and all the power said to be contained within it was too tempting to bear, and many more attempts at stealing the book were made over the years. Another successfully managed to capture the book, and the gods, angered once again, tormented the person. After tormenting them, the person who had the book returned it to the original tomb, and this time, the tomb was sealed for good. This indicates that the knowledge of the gods was not meant for ordinary mortals, and no mortal is meant to decipher and master the secrets of the earth, air, sea, and celestial bodies.

The people at the time were forbidden from being in possession of this knowledge. Over the years, researchers have discovered a connection that exists between the Hall of Records and believes that the book's final resting place for the last 12,000 lies underneath a Sphinx, moved from its original place of burial with Prince Neferkaptah in the City of the Dead. The entrance is beneath the head of the Sphinx, with two known chambers underneath.

The Book of The Dead

A lot of beliefs in ancient Egypt centered around life, death, and the afterlife. In ancient Egypt, no relic is greater than the Book of the Dead. It was a book that very thoroughly illustrated ancient Egypt's funeral traditions and the concept of life and death, including the afterlife that they so greatly believed in. It is not *one* book, but rather a series of transcripts, and it gives an insightful look at what the Egyptians thought about death. It also explains what the ancient Egyptians believed happened after death, and the multitude of spells that they relied on to help them get to the afterlife. The journey to the afterlife was not an easy one.

We call it the Book of the Dead, but the ancient Egyptians had other names for it too. It was essentially a collection of spells, prayers, and incantations; everything that the dead would need in the afterlife. It is a tradition that goes all the way back to the Old Kingdom, and the writings were called the Pyramid Texts, which were a set of instructions for what one needed to do in the afterlife. Sometimes the texts were written on papyrus or shrouds that the dead were buried in. The infamous depiction of Anubis weighing the heart of man comes from the Book of the Dead. These texts were the ancient Egyptians' effort to document the very ancient empire from which the New Kingdom emerged. Papyrus writings during this period were expensive, and it was only the rich who could afford this luxury.

Not only does the book contain details of what happens in the afterlife for an ancient Egyptian, but it also contains information about the gods of Egypt who would judge the Egyptians in this world and the next. The book also contains a vast list of spells that were designed to help a person on their trials in the underworld so that they may be judged worthy enough to enter the afterlife. The Book of the Dead contains the oldest known religious writings in the world.

Every Book of the Dead was uniquely different. The chapters of the book at the time were not arranged in a specific order. Instead, the spells and texts were customized based on the preference of either the relatives of the deceased or the deceased themselves. Approximately 192 spells are known to be contained within the Book of the Dead, with the most renowned one discovered being *The Papyrus of Ani.*

Ani was a scribe from the ancient city of Thebes and lived in the 13th century BCE. Ani had a 78-foot long papyrus scroll of the Book of the Dead. Contained on the scroll was everything he believed he needed to attain immortality. Funerary texts like these were originally written only to be seen by the pharaohs of Egypt, but over time, the Egyptians began to believe that even ordinary people could reach the afterlife if they could succeed in the passage there. Ani's journey began when he died, his body mummified by the priests of the temple who removed every organ in his body. Every organ that is, except his heart. The heart was believed to be where emotion, memories, and intelligence resided. Ani was then wrapped in linen that was woven with charms for protection. A scarab amulet was placed above his heart. The mummification process was meant to preserve Ani's body so that one day his spirit may reunite with the body and become whole again. However, before that can happen, Ani's spirit must pass through the underworld, a realm of magical gates and vast fires that were guarded by beasts that were fearsome. Apophis, the serpent god of darkness, lurked in the shadows, waiting to swallow Ani's soul should he fail in his journey.

Ani was protected, thanks to the magic within the Book of the Dead. Like many Egyptians at the time who could afford to do it, Ani had his scroll customized so that it would contain the spells he believed his spirit would need in the underworld. Armed with this knowledge, Ani was successful in overcoming the challenges of the underworld and repelling any attacks the monsters attempted upon him. He even managed to successfully avoid Apophis to reach the Hall of Ma'at. It is here that Ani would be faced with his final challenge, where he would be judged by 42 assessor gods. These gods would decide if Ani had lived a righteous life. Ani approached each one of the gods, addressing each of the 42 by name and declaring a sin that he did not commit in front of each one. Ani made declarations of innocence, claiming that he has not been an eavesdropper while he was alive, made no one cry, and did not pollute the waters of the river Nile. Did Ani live the perfect life that he wanted the gods to believe? Not really, but that was why he was buried with the scarab above his heart. The scarab, known as the Heart Scarab, had words inscribed upon it which read: *Do not stand as a witness against me.* The words were such so that Ani's heart would not betray him as he made those declarations of innocence in front of the gods. Ani finally reached the moment of truth where he would be judged in front of the god Anubis by weighing his heart on the scale. If Ani's heart was heavier than the feather, weighted down because of his wrongdoings, his heart would be devoured, and Ani would cease to exist. Ani's heart was judged as pure, and Ra took Ani to Osiris, who granted Ani the final approval and permitted him to enter the afterlife.

Should Ani have failed, his soul would have been devoured by Ammit, the soul destroyer. Any soul that was devoured by Ammit meant that there was no chance of ever being reborn. In the afterlife, Ani was reunited with his parents. There is no pain, no sadness, no anger. But in the afterlife, there is still work to be done. Ani, like everyone else there, must work to cultivate a plot of land. Ani is said to be able to do this with the help of a Shabti doll that he was buried with. Today, Ani's papyrus lies in the British Museum, and it has been there since 1888.

After the Book of the Dead was translated by Egyptologists, it became popular as the Bible of the Ancient Egyptians. This translated book can actually be purchased today!

All the spells within the book held the promise that a person's life would continue to exist after they had died. The book helped the relatives of the deceased feel assured that their loved one had found their way to eternal happiness and that they too would be assured of a reward waiting for them at the end if they lived a virtuous life. Texts in the book are both magical and religious, since magic was considered a legitimate activity back then, akin to prayer.

The Egyptians were believers that knowing the name of something meant that you had power over it. In this sense, the book was meant to empower its owner with the mystical names of many of the entities they would encounter in their underworld journey. Like Ani, knowing these names meant that the owner would have power over the entities, thereby enhancing their chances of progressing to the afterlife without having their souls devoured.

Chapter 7: Ancient Sacrifices and Rituals

Like many other cultures around the world, the ancient Egyptians had numerous rituals and sacrifices. It is believed by Egyptologists that the ancient Egyptians practiced human sacrifice. Egypt was no doubt one of the most interesting civilizations in history, filled with rich customs, beliefs, practices, and more. Rituals were performed for all sorts of reasons, like to maintain order and peace in the world, or to protect the dead, seek out help and guidance, and much more. It is no different from today's modern society heading to churches and synagogues or temples to pray and make offerings in the hopes of having prayers answered.

Likewise, offering ceremonies were not an uncommon practice in the Egyptian temples. In fact, daily offerings of weapons, food, tools, carvings, and more were made to the gods on a daily basis. Each ritual would have to be supervised by a priest in the temple. Private rituals that involved evoking mythical powers or events were also performed within the temple walls, and they were usually called upon for protection or healing purposes.

The Egyptian religion was extremely ceremonial and full of rituals that involved daily ceremonial activities. Some of the rituals were complex, and they involved celebrating both the divine and the regular. The Egyptians believed that the rituals were important to both the living as well as the dead. Even death involved several ceremonies and rituals, including the infamous mummification process.

The Mummification Ritual and Burial Customs

Mummies were placed in coffins that were shaped to resemble the form of a man and were often decorated to look like the deceased. When everything had been completed, the coffins would be placed into protective sarcophagus' made of stone. The mummification and embalming process are some of ancient Egypt's best-known rituals and customs.

The ancient Egyptians believed in an afterlife, and that after you died, your spirit lived on. But of course, your spirit needed a place to live; therefore, dead bodies needed to be preserved. The ancient Egyptians developed the art of mummification in 2600 BCE and practiced it for over 3,000 years. The full process was expensive, and only the rich and powerful could afford it. Those with less money had to settle for simpler forms of mummification. If you were among the privileged, the mummification process took around 70 days to complete. The dead body was brought to the embalmer, who wore the mask of Anubis, the Egyptian god of mummification and the afterlife. The body was cleaned, and the liver, lungs, stomach, and intestines were removed to be embalmed separately.

These organs were placed in individual containers called canopic jars and were kept with the mummified body. The brain was seen as having no use and was removed from the skull through the nose using a metal hook. The heart was removed from the body, wrapped in linen, and placed back in the chest. The body was then packed full of and covered with a powdery substance called Natron. Natron looked a lot like baking soda and would dry out the body. After the drying process, which took many days, the body was stuffed to hold its shape and covered inside and out with resin, a sticky substance taken from tree sap. The resin was believed to help preserve the body. Then the body was carefully wrapped in strips of linen fabric, with each of the dead's fingers and toes wrapped separately. The entire wrapping process could take up to two weeks to complete. Because the body would be a home for the spirit, the wrapped mummy could be decorated with jewels, metals, and paint. Royalty would often have an ornate mask placed over the head of their mummy, and gold tips to cover their fingers. Since it was believed the dead lived on in the afterlife, their loved ones wanted to make death comfortable for them.

Many everyday items were buried with mummies; things like food, drink, clothing, utensils, and more. Even mummified pets and servants who were killed and mummified were buried with the dead to serve them. Tombs were built to house the mummies and their possessions. Some mummies were buried in caves and even in the sandy deserts of Egypt. As people began to discover mummies, their tombs were looted and destroyed. Often robbers didn't treat them with respect and unwrapped and destroyed the bodies.

Blood Sacrifices to The Gods

In ancient Egypt, it was the blood sacrifice that was considered the most supreme of all the rituals. Why? Because it was thought to be the most powerful thing that the people could do to appease the gods. At first, it was only animals that were used in sacrificial rituals, like bulls, for example, which were a symbol of the god Taurus. Thus, sacrificing the bull was viewed as a way of presenting the gods with a noble gift, with the bull symbolizing the demigod. Crocodiles, which were seen as a symbolism for Seth, were also used in sacrificial rituals in Dendera and Edfu.

Legend says that over time, the ancient Egyptians began using humans in their sacrificial rituals. Before they were sacrificed, the victims would be honored and treated as though they were gods on earth. Historians believed that those who were commonly sacrificed were either rebels, criminals, or prisoners of war. Criminal sacrifices were thought to be done to appease the goddess Sekmet.

You could say that the servants who were ritualistically put to death on purpose so they could be buried together with their masters were also a form of human sacrifice. Back then, however, the servants who were sacrificed in this manner did not feel as though they were being murdered. The ancient Egyptians certainly had a complicated relationship with death. The servants who were sent to die alongside their masters considered it a privilege at the time, an honor to be able to follow a powerful figure into the afterlife and continue to serve them there.

The Opening of the Mouth Ritual

This ritual was symbolic of reanimating a mummy magically by opening its mouth so that it could breathe, speak, eat, and drink. The Old Kingdom is where evidence of this ritual being practiced has been found. During the ceremony, special tools had to be used. An *adze,* for example, was a special ritual censer shaped to resemble an arm. The *peseshkaf* was a spooned blade that was also commonly used in these rituals, along with an assortment of other amulets. Egyptians back then believed that if your soul was to have any chance of survival in the afterlife, you needed to have food and water. By opening the mouth in this ritual, it meant that even in death, you could still do what you needed to do to survive.

Cleopatra's Beauty Rituals

Cleopatra's beauty rituals are probably as famed as her beauty. It is still talked about even today, with many beauty gurus and regiments touting Cleopatra as their source. One of her best-known beauty secrets was the fact that she regularly bathed in milk, which was said to help keep her skin soft and beautiful. At room temperature, the milk is fermented by the bacteria within it, and that produces lactic acid. Lactic acid is a powerful ingredient and, in today's skincare world, a popular one too since it is marketed as an ingredient that helps to prevent acne breakouts and reduce the appearance of fine lines and wrinkles, as well as combat other signs of aging. According to Hippocrates, the queen would use the milk of 700 donkeys to bath in, with the lactic acid contained within the milk working as an exfoliating ingredient.

With access to sea salt mined from the caves, the queen was said to also regularly use sea salt as part of her beauty ritual. Royal jelly was another ingredient she favored since it was believed that royal jelly could help the body's cells heal themselves naturally. Indeed, so great was her influence that even thousands of years after her death, her beauty rituals are still being talked about and copied today.

The Ways of The Priests

In Egypt, every town or city had at least one temple, but surprisingly, most of the population never actually stepped foot inside most of the temples. It was thought that only the pharaohs and his priests should be allowed to enter the sacred home of the gods. Priests were very important figures in the temples of ancient Egypt, and they had many responsibilities, including performing many of the elaborate rituals that were practiced during that time. The priests would begin their day by removing the hair from their head and body after bathing in the sacred lake of the temple. They would then dress in clean white linen, a symbolism of being pure while they were in the presence of the mighty gods.

Strange, Little Known Facts About Ancient Egypt

It is safe to say that the ancient Egyptians were way ahead of their time in many ways. It was a kingdom of many secrets and interesting facts. Some of the most interesting are listed below:

- **Pharaohs Were Not as Slim as They Were Portrayed** - The hieroglyphic paintings might depict the pharaoh's as being slim and fit, but the truth was, many of the pharaohs at the time were overweight. This could be attributed to the lavish lifestyle they led, where food, drink, and offerings were in abundance. The pharaohs were offered meat, fruit, honey, cake, wine, beer, and many more luxury decadences. Queen Hatshepsut's mummy proves that royalty might not have been as accurately depicted in the old artwork as we were led to believe.

- **It Wasn't the Slaves Who Built the Pyramids** - The pyramids are no doubt one of Egypt's most recognizable relics, but contrary to popular belief, they were not built by the slaves at all. They were, in fact, built by skilled construction workers, and they were paid for their services. This workforce is believed to have been comprised primarily of farmers who could not work during the flood season.

- **Equality for Women** - The women in ancient Egypt were given equal treatment to that of the men. The gods and goddesses of Egypt were seen as equally powerful, so it comes as no surprise that the women were viewed as equal to the men on earth. A testament to this fact is how some of the greatest pharaohs and leaders in Egypt were women, like Cleopatra, for example.

- **The Men Wore Makeup Too** - It wasn't only the women in Egypt who cared about their appearance. The men did too. They did not necessarily wear makeup for vanity, though. Instead, it was believed that makeup had "healing magic," and they would apply Kohl liner around their eyes using a liner that was made out of bone, wood, and ivory.

- **The Old Kingdom's "Fly King"** - A little known fact about Egypt is how the old Kingdom was home to Pepi II, the last pharaoh of the Old Kingdom. He also happened to be known as the "Fly King" because of his hatred for flies. It is said that he would have slaves smear honey around him as an attempt to keep the flies away.

- **They had Citizens Rights** - King Menes combined the Upper and Lower Kingdoms in 2500 BC, and it was at this time that the empire's first laws began to emerge. While the pharaoh continued to maintain his supreme power over everything, everyone was treated with equality in the kingdom. Men and women had the same rights, and in general, it didn't matter which social class you were in, you still were treated fairly as long as you were not a slave. Even the poorest of Egypt's citizens had the right to ask the Vizier for help if they needed it.

- **No Forced Marriages** - The women in ancient Egypt could choose who they wanted for a husband. They even got to decide if they wanted to get married or remain single. They could sign contracts, own property, take legal action, and inherit belongings the same way that the men could. The women could even get paid jobs if they wanted, and it was not uncommon for many of the women to hold influential positions at the top society, as Hatshepsut and Cleopatra did. They were only allowed to have secondary positions in temples, though.

- **Polygamy Was Allowed** - King Tutankhamen was known for marrying his half-sister and several other wives. The idea of polygamy was not common, but it was allowed.

- **Fairly Advanced Treatments and Medicines** - The ancient Egyptians had fairly advanced treatments and medicines compared to a lot of other civilizations that existed around the same time. Strangely though, they believed that laxatives were the answer to most ailments. Laxatives at the time were made with a range of ingredients, like bran, figs, dates, castor oil, and a fruit called colocynth. The Egyptians also believed that illnesses had a spiritual component to them, and thus, they would combine their understanding of how the human body worked with various incantations and rituals. Spells were cast to encourage healing while at the same time warding off spirits.

- **Strict Rules for Criminal Punishment** - The Egyptians had strict rules when it came to being punished for your crimes. Back then, the pharaohs were the ones who decided how the criminals or those found guilty of a crime should be punished. If the pharaoh was not available, the job would fall to a Vizier or an Oracle. Punishments were either fatal or non-fatal. Jails were not prevalent at the time, and if you committed a crime, you were punished for it and then sent to resume your normal way of life. Punishments ranged from lashes to being exiled, sometimes even disfigurement. Grave robbing, which was an unforgivable crime, would be punished by drowning, impalement, or decapitation. If you were caught vandalizing a temple, you would be burned alive. This was the worst punishment imaginable since burning took away the person's body, which meant that they would not have been able to enter the afterlife.

- **The Mummification Process Didn't Happen Right Away** - When a person died, they were not taken to be mummified straight away. Instead, the deceased was only taken to the mummification chambers a few days after they had passed away. The reason for this was to prevent unscrupulous workers from taking advantage of the deceased, especially the ones who were attractive.

- **Animals Were Buried Too** - Since animals played such a major role in the life of the ancient Egyptians, they were mummified the same way that people were. This included falcons and hippos, not just cats and dogs, and other household pets. Most remains that were found were cats, although dogs and monkeys were also discovered over the years. Some animals were even buried with amulets that would keep them safe in the afterlife. One discovery in the City of the Dead found eight million mummified puppies, which were thought to have been preserved by an animal cult that worshipped Anubis.

- **They Didn't Ride Camels** – Another interesting fact about the people back then was that camels *were not* their main mode of transport. In fact, they didn't ride them at all. They preferred donkeys for traveling and the transport of goods. Besides donkeys, boats were the other common mode of transportation. They would fill the larger boats with heavy blocks of stone and grain. The smaller, lightweight boats made of papyrus were the ones that carried the people up and down the river. The Nile was a river that flowed directly through the middle of the land, which meant that the Nile was a natural highway. With the current, it allowed the people to easily move from north to south and vice versa. The strong winds pushed the boats along, making boat travel almost effortless.

- **There Were 1,400 Different Gods and Goddesses** – More than 1,400 various gods and goddesses were worshipped by the people of the time besides Ra, Isis, Osiris, and Bastet.

- **The Djoser Is the Oldest Pyramid** – The Djoser pyramids are believed to be the oldest ones in Egypt, and they were built sometime in 27th century BC. Buried inside the pyramids were nobility and their prized possessions. The people were firm believers in taking your belongings with you in the afterlife because you would need them. Another interesting fact about the pyramids is how they were built along the Nile's west banks, where the sun would set. The setting sun was believed to relate to the realm of the dead. Each pyramid took roughly 200 years to build, which meant multiple pyramids were often constructed around the same time. This would explain why there are so many in Egypt despite the absence of modern technology to speed up the process.

- **Giza Is the Most Famous Pyramid in History -** No pyramid's name is more recognizable than that of Giza. It is probably the most famous of all the structures in Egypt. It served as a giant tomb when it was completed. The Pyramid of Giza held the record as the biggest structure that existed in the world that was man-made, a record it would hold for thousands of years until 1311. It was then surpassed by the Lincoln Cathedral, but the cathedral didn't hold the record for long since the central spire collapsed sometime in 1548. The Great Pyramid of Giza is the only one of the original seven wonders of the world that still exists intact. The other six wonders like the Colossus of Rhodes, the Statue of Zeus, the Lighthouse of Alexandria, and the Hanging Gardens of

Babylon were destroyed or damaged over time. But if you travel to Egypt, you will still be able to see this Great Pyramid. Unfortunately, the Great Pyramid also happens to be sinking into the sand. The pyramid was built over 4,000 years ago with limestone and granite blocks, and since then, natural erosion over the years caused it to sink 25-feet into the ground.

- **The Believed Animals Were Incarnations of the Gods -** The ancient Egyptians believed in a lot of things, including the fact that the animals of the land were incarnations of the gods they believed in. The ancient Egyptians were one of the very first civilizations that kept animals as pets, especially cats. They adored cats, and they would often mummify their beloved pets and bury them with their owners. Other animals that the people held a deep respect for were lions, ibises, hawks, and baboons, which were why sometimes the gods were depicted as half man and half beast. Cats were kept as pets while the other animals were trained for work.

- **They Loved Playing Board Games** – For ancient Egyptians, this was a fun way to pass the time. One popular game was called *Mehen,* and it was made of a stone board. The board was carved to resemble a coiled snake. It is uncertain what the rules of the game were, though. Another popular game that was played at the time was called *Senet,* which was a game of chance. We know for certain this was a popular game, especially among royalty since there were depictions discovered of Queen Nefertiti playing the game. Even King Tut was discovered buried with a *Senet* board. The *Senet* was a game played on a longboard that consisted of 30 painted squares. The players of the game had to move the pieces along based on dice throws.

- **The Sleeping Arrangements Weren't Great** – Instead of a pillow, what the people would use at that time was a headrest that would sit uncomfortably high on the bed. The Egyptians chose to sleep this way, believing that since the head was the body's spiritual center, it had to be protected, and these headrests would do the job. The headrest was reserved for only the wealthiest of the people who could afford such a luxury.

- **King Tut Was Embalmed Without His Heart** – Something unusual about King Tut was the way that the boy king was embalmed without his heart. Based on what we know, this was extremely unusual, especially for one who was a pharaoh. The speculation around this is that the young king probably suffered a severe injury. One that was enough to damage his heart and make it almost impossible to preserve. The Egyptians loved hunting, and a hippopotamus was one of the many animals they would hunt for sport. King Tut's tomb even has depictions of him flinging harpoons at them. Because of this, some scholars believe that his cause of death may have been a hunt that went very wrong.

- **Cleopatra Might Not Have Been as Beautiful as Today's Depictions** - There is some evidence which points to the fact that Cleopatra may not have been as attractive as history has led us to believe. Coins with the famous queen's face have been discovered, but looking at them, you wouldn't think that it was the queen at all. The coins depict Cleopatra as having masculine features with a very large nose, although some historians believe this was done on purpose as a show of strength.

- **The City That Sank into the Ocean** - No, it wasn't Atlantis, this time it was Heracleion, a city in ancient Egypt. The original metropolis was built on a group of islands that were located near the Nile. It was one of Egypt's main international trading ports, probably founded sometime in 1200 BC. Back then, it flourished around 600 BC, and it was only 600 years later that it would sink. Since the city was built after an earthquake, this probably happened because of liquefaction. Many historians considered this city a myth until one French archaeologist found it in 2000, proving that the city did, in fact, exist. The archaeologist who made this very interesting discovery claims that they are only at the start of their research, and there is more to be found.

- **The Mystery of the Sphinx's Missing Nose** – A popular theory that circles around the mystery of the missing nose is that it was shot off by Napoleon's men in 1798 when they conquered Egypt. However, sketches discovered of the statue in 1737 already show that the nose was missing, and this was 60 years before Napoleon even arrived in Egypt.

- Hieroglyphics Were Not the Main Language - Although hieroglyphics are arguably the most famous and recognizable of the ancient Egyptian writings, thanks largely to the focus and attention given by Hollywood movies like *The Mummy,* hieroglyphs were not the main language at the time. They were actually only used for official inscriptions and during rituals. The everyday language used for writing was the *hieratic*, which made a lot more sense. There were so many different hieroglyphs that using it daily would have been far too confusing and inconvenient.

Conclusion

Thank you for making it through to the end of *Egyptian Mythology*! I hope it was informative and able to answer many of the questions you may have had about Ancient Egypt.

Ancient Egypt is easily one of the most influential societies to ever exist in this world, so powerful in fact, that we still think about it and talk about it today! It continues to influence modern movies, books, and TV shows. And of course, countless numbers of people travel to Egypt each year just to see the great pyramids.

Egypt's tales of enthralling gods, magic, captivating rituals, rich stories, and the concepts of reincarnation and life after death are unlike any other civilization in the world. To the Egyptians, your existence here on earth was only a small part of your journey. They believed that your existence on earth was *part* of your overall eternal journey, simply preparing you for greater things to come.

Indeed, ancient Egypt has left the world enthralled, and it will continue to do so for many years to come. Discoveries continue to be made in that part of the world even today, and there's no doubt that more intriguing information and mysteries will continue to be unraveled. The reign of old Egypt may have been over for thousands of years, but the rich legacy that it leaves behind will never disappear.

Thanks again for taking the time to read this book. I hope you have thoroughly enjoyed learning about Ancient Egypt and Egyptian mythology! If you're interested in learning more about other mythologies, please keep your eye out for my other books available on Amazon as well as through a variety of other distributors. Currently, these titles cover the topics of Celtic, Norse, and Greek mythology.

www.ingramcontent.com/pod-product-compliance
Lightning Source LLC
LaVergne TN
LVHW011724060526
838200LV00051B/3009